Exercises for
A Canadian Writer's Reference

Fifth Edition

Diana Hacker

Nancy Sommers
Harvard University

Bedford / St. Martin's   Boston ◆ New York

Manufactured in the United States of America.

6   5   4   3

f   e

For information, write: Bedford/St. Martin's,
75 Arlington Street, Boston, MA 02116
(617-399-4000)

ISBN: 978-0-312-57116-0

A Note for Instructors

The exercise sets in this booklet are keyed to specific sections in *A Canadian Writer's Reference*. If you have adopted *A Canadian Writer's Reference* as a text, you are welcome to photocopy any or all of these exercises for a variety of possible uses:

- as homework
- as classroom practice
- as quizzes
- as individualized self-teaching assignments
- as support for a writing centre or learning lab

This exercise booklet is also available for student purchase.

The exercises are double-spaced, and the instructions ask students to edit the sentences with cross-outs and insertions, not simply to recopy them with corrections. Students will thus receive practice in the same editing techniques they are expected to apply in their own drafts.

Most exercise sets begin with an example that is done for the student, followed by five lettered sentences for which answers are provided in the back of the booklet. The sets then continue with five numbered sentences whose answers are given in the instructor's answer key only. If you would like students to work independently, checking all of their revisions themselves, you may of course reproduce the answer key.

A Note for Students

The exercises in this booklet accompany the grammar coverage in *A Canadian Writer's Reference*. To benefit from the exercises, you may find it helpful to first read the corresponding section in the book (such as S1, Parallelism), which is illustrated with sentences similar to those in the exercises.

Most of the exercise sets consist of five lettered sentences and five numbered sentences. Answers to the lettered sentences appear in the back of this booklet so that you may test your understanding without the help of an instructor. Instructors use the numbered sentences for a variety of purposes—as homework or as quizzes, for example. If your instructor prefers that you use all of the exercise sentences for self-study, he or she may provide you with an answer key to both the lettered and the numbered sentences.

All exercises are double-spaced so that you can edit the sentences with cross-outs and insertions instead of recopying whole sentences. *A Canadian Writer's Reference* shows you how to edit, and a sample sentence at the beginning of each exercise set demonstrates the technique. Many writers edit on hard copy. For these exercises, you will find that editing has three important advantages over recopying: It is much faster, it allows you to focus on the problem at hand, and it prevents you from introducing new errors as you revise.

Contents

Sentence Style

Word Choice

Grammatical Sentences

Multilingual Writers and ESL Challenges

Punctuation and Mechanics

Basic Grammar

EXERCISE S1-1 ◆ Parallelism

Before working this exercise, read section S1 in *A Canadian Writer's Reference*, Fifth Edition.

Edit the following sentences to correct faulty parallelism. Revisions of lettered sentences appear in the back of the booklet. Example:

checking
Rowena began her workday by pouring a cup of coffee and ~~checked~~ her e-mail.
                                                                      ^

a. Police dogs are used for finding lost children, tracking criminals, and the detection of bombs and illegal drugs.

b. Hannah told her rock-climbing partner that she bought a new harness and of her desire to climb Mount McConnell.

c. It is more difficult to sustain an exercise program than starting one.

d. During basic training, I was not only told what to do but also what to think.

e. Jan wanted to drive to the wine country or at least the Niagara Escarpment.

1. Camp activities include fishing trips, dance lessons, and computers.

2. Arriving at Grand Lake in a thunderstorm, the campers found it safer to remain in their cars than setting up their tents.

3. The streets were not only too steep but also were too narrow for anything other than pedestrian traffic.

4. More digital artists in the show are from South Vancouver than North Vancouver.

5. To load her toolbox, Anika the Clown gathered hats of different sizes, put in two tubes of face paint, arranged a bundle of extra-long straws, added a bag of coloured balloons, and a battery-powered hair dryer.

Hacker/Sommers, *Exercises for A Canadian Writer's Reference*, 5th ed. (Boston: Bedford, 2012)

S1-1 | Parallelism   **1**

EXERCISE S2-1 ◆ Needed words

Before working this exercise, read section S2 in *A Canadian Writer's Reference*, Fifth Edition.

Add any words needed for grammatical or logical completeness in the following sentences. Revisions of lettered sentences appear in the back of the booklet. Example:

> *that*
> **The officer feared the prisoner would escape.**
>   ^

a.   A grapefruit or orange is a good source of vitamin C.

b.   The women entering RMC can expect haircuts as short as the male cadets.

c.   Looking out the family room window, Sarah saw her favourite tree, which she had climbed as a child, was gone.

d.   The graphic designers are interested and knowledgeable about producing posters for the balloon race.

e.   Reefs are home to more species than any ecosystem in the sea.

1.   Dr. Anderson Abbott, the first Black Canadian licensed doctor, fought in the US Civil War and faced more severe restrictions than white doctors.

2.   Rachel is interested and committed to working at a school in Ecuador next semester.

3.   Vassily likes mathematics more than his teacher.

4.   The inspection team saw many historic buildings had been damaged by the earthquake.

5.   Lila knows seven languages, but she found English harder to learn than any language.

Hacker/Sommers, *Exercises for A Canadian Writer's Reference*, 5th ed. (Boston: Bedford, 2012)

EXERCISE S3-1 ◆ Misplaced modifiers

Before working this exercise, read sections S3-a to S3-d in *A Canadian Writer's Reference*, Fifth Edition.

Edit the following sentences to correct misplaced or awkwardly placed modifiers. Revisions of lettered sentences appear in the back of the booklet. Example:

> *in a telephone survey*
> **Answering questions can be annoying. ~~in a telephone survey.~~**
>   ^   ^

a. More research is needed to effectively evaluate the risks posed by volcanoes in the Pacific Northwest.

b. Many students graduate with debt from university totalling more than twenty thousand dollars.

c. It is a myth that humans only use 10 percent of their brains.

d. A coolhunter is a person who can find in the unnoticed corners of modern society the next wave of fashion.

e. All geese do not fly beyond Kamloops for the winter.

1. The flood nearly displaced half of the city's residents, who packed into several overcrowded shelters.

2. Most lions at night hunt for medium-size prey, such as zebra.

3. Several recent studies have encouraged heart patients to more carefully watch their cholesterol levels.

4. The garden's centrepiece is a huge sculpture that was carved by three women called *Walking in Place*.

5. The old Marlboro ads depicted a man on a horse smoking a cigarette.

Hacker/Sommers, *Exercises for A Canadian Writer's Reference,* 5th ed. (Boston: Bedford, 2012)

S3-1 | Misplaced modifiers   **3**

EXERCISE S3-2 ◆ Dangling modifiers

Before working this exercise, read section S3-e in *A Canadian Writer's Reference*, Fifth Edition.

Edit the following sentences to correct dangling modifiers. Most sentences can be revised in more than one way. Revisions of lettered sentences appear in the back of the booklet. Example:

> *a student must complete*
> **To acquire a degree in almost any field, two science courses. must be completed.**
> ^ ^

a. Though only sixteen, UBC accepted Martha's application.

b. To replace the gear mechanism, attached is a form to order the part by mail.

c. Settled in the cockpit, the pounding of the engine was muffled only slightly by my helmet.

d. After studying polymer chemistry, computer games seemed less complex to Phuong.

e. When a young man, my mother enrolled me in tap dance classes.

1. While working as a warden in Glacier National Park, a grizzly bear crossed the road in front of my truck one night.

2. By following the new recycling procedure, the city's landfill costs will be reduced significantly.

3. Serving as president of the missionary circle, one of Sophia's duties is to raise money for the church.

4. After buying an album by Ali Farka Toure, the rich and rolling rhythms of Malian music made more sense to Silas.

5. Opening the window to let out a huge bumblebee, the car swerved into an oncoming truck.

Hacker/Sommers, *Exercises for A Canadian Writer's Reference*, 5th ed. (Boston: Bedford, 2012)

EXERCISE S4-1 ◆ Shifts: point of view

Before working this exercise, read section S4-a in *A Canadian Writer's Reference*, Fifth Edition.

Edit the following paragraph to eliminate distracting shifts in point of view (person and number).

When online dating first became available, many people thought that it would simplify romance. We believed that you could type in a list of criteria—sense of humour, university education, green eyes, good job—and a database would select the perfect mate. Thousands of people signed up for services and filled out their profiles, confident that true love was only a few mouse clicks away. As it turns out, however, virtual dating is no easier than traditional dating. I still have to contact the people I find, exchange e-mails and phone calls, and meet him in the real world. Although a database might produce a list of possibilities and screen out obviously undesirable people, you can't predict chemistry. More often than not, people who seem perfect online just don't click in person. Electronic services do help a single person expand their pool of potential dates, but it's no substitute for the hard work of romance.

EXERCISE S4-2 ◆ Shifts: tense

Before working this exercise, read section S4-b in *A Canadian Writer's Reference*, Fifth Edition.

Edit the following paragraphs to eliminate distracting shifts in tense.

Settling Canada was arduous. Until 1608, many European attempts at permanent settlements—at Sable Island, Tadoussac, and Port Royal, for example—failed.

The first successful settlement begins on July 3, 1608, when Samuel de Champlain founded Quebec for France. Although Champlain formed an alliance with the Algonquian and Montagnais peoples, survival is still difficult. To help his settlers develop skills, Champlain sends men to live with the Aboriginal peoples. These men were known as the *coureurs de bois* (runners of the woods).

Twenty-eight people originally settled Quebec. By 1630, the number had risen to only one hundred. The *coureurs de bois* extend the French influence to the Huron peoples in the Great Lakes area, but the English colonies in the region were stronger. To bolster the French colony, in 1627 Cardinal Richelieu, regent of France, founded the Company of 100 Associates. He gives land to people to settle in New France and names Champlain governor.

Champlain was a prolific writer. He spent 1629 to 1632 writing a seven-hundred-page book called *Les voyages de la nouvelle France occidentale, dicte Canada faits par le Sr de Champlain*. In his works, Champlain reveals nothing about himself; his meticulous descriptions of what he did and saw contained no value judgments and opinions. Thus his works are the best account we had of the beginnings of Canadian history.

Hacker/Sommers, *Exercises for A Canadian Writer's Reference*, 5th ed. (Boston: Bedford, 2012)

EXERCISE S4-3 ◆ Shifts: mood and voice, questions and quotations

Before working this exercise, read sections S4-c and S4-d in *A Canadian Writer's Reference*, Fifth Edition.

Edit the following sentences to make the verbs consistent in mood and voice and to eliminate distracting shifts from indirect to direct questions or quotations. Revisions of lettered sentences appear in the back of the booklet. Example:

> **As a public relations intern, I wrote press releases, managed the Web site, and**
> *fielded all phone calls.*
> ~~all phone calls were fielded by me.~~
> ^

a. A talented musician, Julie Crochetière uses R&B, soul, and jazz styles. Even pop music is performed well by her.

b. Environmentalists point out that shrimp farming in Southeast Asia is polluting water and making farmlands useless. They warn that action must be taken by governments before it is too late.

c. The samples were observed for five days before we detected any growth.

d. In his famous soliloquy, Hamlet contemplates whether death would be preferable to his difficult life and, if so, is he capable of committing suicide?

e. The lawyer told the judge that Miranda Hale was innocent and allow her to prove the allegations false.

1. When the photographs were taken on the beach at sunset, I intentionally left the foreground out of focus.

2. If the warning sirens sound, evacuate at once. It is not advised that you return to the building until the alarm has stopped.

3. Most baby products warn parents not to leave children unattended. Also, follow all directions carefully.

4. The advertisement promised that results would be seen in five days or consumers could return the product for a full refund.

5. Investigators need to determine whether there was a forcible entry and then what was the motive?

Hacker/Sommers, *Exercises for A Canadian Writer's Reference*, 5th ed. (Boston: Bedford, 2012)

S4-3 | Shifts: mood and voice, questions and quotations   **7**

EXERCISE S4-4 ◆ Shifts

Before working this exercise, read section S4 in *A Canadian Writer's Reference*, Fifth Edition.

Edit the following sentences to eliminate distracting shifts. Revisions of lettered sentences appear in the back of the booklet. Example:

> **For many first-year engineering students, adjusting to a rigorous course load can be so**
> *they*
> **challenging that ~~you~~ sometimes feel overwhelmed.**
>   ^

a. A courtroom lawyer has more than a touch of theatre in their blood.

b. The interviewer asked if we had brought our proof of citizenship and did we bring our passports?

c. The reconnaissance scout often has to make fast decisions and use sophisticated equipment to keep their team from being detected.

d. After the animators finish their scenes, the production designer arranges the clips according to the storyboard. Synchronization notes must also be made for the sound editor and the composer.

e. Madame Defarge is a sinister figure in Dickens's *A Tale of Two Cities*. On a symbolic level, she represents fate; like the Greek Fates, she knitted the fabric of individual destiny.

1. Everyone should protect yourself from the sun, especially on the first day of extensive exposure.

2. Our neighbours told us that the island was being evacuated because of the coming storm. Also, take the northern route to the mainland.

3. Rescue workers put water on her face and lifted her head gently onto a pillow. Finally, she opens her eyes.

4. In my first tai chi class, the instructor asked if I had ever done yoga stretches and did I have good balance?

5. The artist has often been seen as a threat to society, especially when they refuse to conform to conventional standards of taste.

Hacker/Sommers, *Exercises for A Canadian Writer's Reference*, 5th ed. (Boston: Bedford, 2012)

EXERCISE S5-1 ◆ Mixed constructions

Before working this exercise, read section S5 in *A Canadian Writer's Reference*, Fifth Edition.

Edit the following sentences to untangle mixed constructions. Revisions of lettered sentences appear in the back of the booklet. Example:

> *Taking*
> ~~By taking~~ the oath of citizenship made Ling a Canadian citizen.
> ^

a. Using surgical gloves is a precaution now worn by dentists to prevent contact with patients' blood and saliva.

b. A physician, the career my brother is pursuing, requires at least ten years of challenging work.

c. The reason the pharaohs had bad teeth was because tiny particles of sand found their way into Egyptian bread.

d. Recurring bouts of flu among team members set a record for number of games forfeited.

e. In this box contains the key to your future.

1. Early diagnosis of prostate cancer is often curable.

2. Depending on our method of travel and our destination determines how many suitcases we are allowed to take.

3. Dyslexia is where people have a learning disorder that impairs reading ability.

4. Even though Ellen had heard French spoken all her life, yet she could not speak it.

5. In understanding artificial intelligence code is a critical skill for computer game designers.

Hacker/Sommers, *Exercises for A Canadian Writer's Reference*, 5th ed. (Boston: Bedford, 2012)

S5-1 | Mixed constructions **9**

EXERCISE S6-1 ◆ Coordination and subordination

Before working this exercise, read section S6-a in *A Canadian Writer's Reference*, Fifth Edition.

Use the coordination or subordination technique in brackets to combine each pair of independent clauses. Revisions of lettered sentences appear in the back of the booklet. Example:

> *baseball, but he*
> **Ferguson Jenkins was one of the best pitchers in the history of ~~baseball. He~~ never won**
> ^
> **a World Series ring.** [Use a comma and a coordinating conjunction.]

a.   In 1987, Jenkins was elected to the Canadian Baseball Hall of Fame. He was the first Canadian elected to the Baseball Hall of Fame in Cooperstown, New York. [Use a comma and a coordinating conjunction.]

b.   Jenkins was the first Canadian pitcher to win the Cy Young Award. He also won the Lou Marsh Trophy as Canada's outstanding athlete in 1974. [Use a semicolon.]

c.   Jenkins was grateful to have won a Cy Young Award. Jenkins felt that he should have won more. [Use the subordinating conjunction *although*.]

d.   Jenkins loved being a baseball pitcher. He told *Baseball Almanac* that he didn't consider pitching to be work. [Use a semicolon and the transitional phrase *for example*.]

e.   Jenkins pitched six consecutive twenty-win seasons between 1967 and 1972. He will likely be the last pitcher to do it because today's pitchers start fewer games. [Use a semicolon.]

1.   In 1967, Jenkins was elected to his first All-Star game. He threw six strikeouts in three innings in that game. [Use a comma and a coordinating conjunction.]

2.   Jenkins was named Canadian male athlete of the year four times. He was listed as one of the top one hundred baseball players of the twentieth century by the Society for American Baseball Research. [Use the relative pronoun *who*.]

3.   Jenkins threw his forty-ninth career shutout in 1983. That year he retired as a player. [Use a semicolon.]

4.   In 2000, Jenkins started the Fergie Jenkins Foundation. It raises money to support local charities. [Use the relative pronoun *which*.]

5. At the 1995 All-Star game, Ferguson Jenkins returned as the National League honorary pitching coach. His team won the game. [Use a comma and a coordinating conjunction.]

Hacker/Sommers, *Exercises for A Canadian Writer's Reference*, 5th ed. (Boston: Bedford, 2012)

EXERCISE S6-2 ◆ Coordination and subordination

Before working this exercise, read section S6-b in *A Canadian Writer's Reference*, Fifth Edition.

Combine the following sentences by subordinating minor ideas or by coordinating ideas of equal importance. You must decide which ideas are minor because the sentences are given out of context. Revisions of lettered sentences appear in the back of the booklet. Example:

> **Agnes, ~~was~~ another girl I taught/, ~~She~~ was a hyperactive child.**

a. The X-Men comic books and Japanese woodcuts of kabuki dancers were part of Marlena's research project on popular culture. They covered the tabletop and the chairs.

b. Our waitress was costumed in a kimono. She had painted her face white. She had arranged her hair in a lacquered beehive.

c. Students can apply for a spot in the leadership program. The program teaches thinking and communication skills.

d. Shore houses were flooded up to the first floor. Beaches were washed away. Brant's Lighthouse was swallowed by the sea.

e. Laura Thackray is an engineer at Volvo Car Corporation. She addressed women's safety needs. She designed a pregnant crash-test dummy.

1. I noticed that the sky was glowing orange and red. I bent down to crawl into the bunker.

2. The Market Inn is located on North Wharf. It doesn't look very impressive from the outside. The food, however, is excellent.

3. He walked up to the pitcher's mound. He dug his toe into the ground. He swung his arm around backward and forward. Then he threw the ball and struck the batter out.

4. Eryn and Maeve have decided to start a business. They have known each other since kindergarten. They will renovate homes for people with disabilities.

5. The first football card set was released by the Goudey Gum Company in 1933. The set featured only three football players. They were Red Grange, Bronko Nagurski, and Knute Rockne.

Hacker/Sommers, *Exercises for A Canadian Writer's Reference*, 5th ed. (Boston: Bedford, 2012)

S6-2 | Coordination and subordination **13**

EXERCISE S6-3 ◆ Coordination and subordination

Before working this exercise, read sections S6-a and S6-c in *A Canadian Writer's Reference*, Fifth Edition.

The following sentences show coordinated ideas (ideas joined with a coordinating conjunction or a semicolon). Restructure the sentences by subordinating minor ideas. You must decide which ideas are minor because the sentences are given out of context. Revisions of lettered sentences appear in the back of the booklet. Example:

> *where they*   *to celebrate*
> The rowers finally returned to shore, ~~and~~ had a party on the beach ~~and celebrated~~
>   ^   ^
> the start of the season.

a. These particles are known as "stealth liposomes," and they can hide in the body for a long time without detection.

b. Jan is a competitive gymnast and majors in biology; her goal is to apply her athletic experience and her science degree to a career in sports medicine.

c. Textile workers and labour unions have loudly protested sweatshop abuses, so apparel makers have been forced to examine their labour practices.

d. IRC (Internet Relay Chat) was developed in a European university; it was created as a way for a group of graduate students to talk about projects from their dorm rooms.

e. The cafeteria's new menu has an international flavour, and it includes everything from enchiladas and pizza to pad thai and sauerbraten.

1. Victor switched on his remote-control lawn mower, and it began to shudder and emit clouds of smoke.

2. Iguanas are dependent on ultraviolet rays from the sun, so in the winter months they must be put under ultraviolet-coated lights that can be purchased at most pet stores.

3. Heritage Canada was founded in 1973; it spearheads a nationwide campaign to preserve significant historic buildings.

4. We did not expect to receive so many large orders so quickly, and we are short on inventory.

5. Mother spread her love equally among us all, but she made each of us feel special in our own way.

Hacker/Sommers, *Exercises for A Canadian Writer's Reference*, 5th ed. (Boston: Bedford, 2012)

EXERCISE S6-4 ◆ Faulty subordination

Before working this exercise, read sections S6-d and S6-e in *A Canadian Writer's Reference*, Fifth Edition.

In each of the following sentences, the idea that the writer wanted to emphasize is buried in a subordinate construction. Restructure each sentence so that the independent clause expresses the major idea, as indicated in brackets, and lesser ideas are subordinated. Revisions of lettered sentences appear in the back of the booklet. Example:

> *Although*
> **Catherine has weathered many hardships, ~~although~~ she has rarely become**
> **^**
>
> **discouraged.** [Emphasize that Catherine has rarely become discouraged.]

a. Gina worked as an aide for the relief agency, distributing food and medical supplies.

    [Emphasize distributing food and medical supplies.]

b. Janbir spent every Saturday learning tabla drumming, noticing each week that his memory

    for complex patterns was growing stronger. [Emphasize Janbir's memory.]

c. The rotor hit, gouging a hole about five centimetres deep in my helmet. [Emphasize that the

    rotor gouged a hole in the helmet.]

d. My grandfather, who raised his daughters the old-fashioned way, was born eighty years ago

    in Puerto Rico. [Emphasize how the grandfather raised his daughters.]

e. The Narcan reversed the depressive effect of the drug, saving the patient's life. [Emphasize

    that the patient's life was saved.]

1. My cousin Fatima, who studied Persian miniature painting after university, majored in

    early childhood education. [Emphasize Fatima's studies after university.]

2. I was losing consciousness when my will to live kicked in. [Emphasize the will to live.]

3. Using a sliding compound mitre saw, the carpenter made intricate edges on the cabinets.

    [Emphasize the carpenter's use of the saw.]

4. Ernie was using origami to solve some tricky manufacturing problems when he decided to

    leave engineering and become an artist. [Emphasize Ernie's decision.]

5. As the undulating waves glinted in the sun, the paddlers synchronized their strokes.

    [Emphasize the brightness of the waves.]

Hacker/Sommers, *Exercises for A Canadian Writer's Reference*, 5th ed. (Boston: Bedford, 2012)

S6-4 | Faulty subordination **15**

EXERCISE S7-1 ◆ Sentence variety

Before working this exercise, read section S7 in *A Canadian Writer's Reference*, Fifth Edition.

Improve sentence variety in each of the following sentences by using the technique suggested in brackets. Revisions of lettered sentences appear in the back of the booklet. Example:

> *To protect endangered marine turtles, fishing*
> ~~Fishing~~ crews place turtle excluder devices in fishing nets. ~~to protect endangered~~
> ^   ^
> ~~marine turtles.~~ [Begin the sentence with the adverbial infinitive phrase.]

a. The exhibits for insects and spiders are across the hall from the fossils exhibit. [Invert the sentence.]

b. Sayuri becomes a successful geisha after growing up desperately poor in Japan. [Move the adverb phrase to the beginning of the sentence.]

c. Researchers have been studying Mount St. Helens for years. They believe that a series of earthquakes in the area may have caused the 1980 eruption. [Combine the sentences into a complex sentence. See also B4-a.]

d. Ice cream typically contains 10 percent milk fat. Premium ice cream may contain up to 16 percent milk fat and has considerably less air in the product. [Combine the two sentences as a compound sentence. See also B4-a.]

e. The economy may recover more quickly than expected if home values climb. [Move the adverb clause to the beginning of the sentence.]

1. The Dust Bowl farmers, looking wearily into the cameras of government photographers, represented the harshest effects of the Great Depression. [Move the participial phrase to the beginning of the sentence.]

2. The Trans Alaska Pipeline was completed in 1977. It has moved more than fifteen billion barrels of oil since 1977. [Combine the two sentences into a complex sentence. See also B4-a.]

3. Mr. Guo habitually dresses in loose clothing and canvas shoes for his wushu workout. [Move the adverb to the beginning of the sentence.]

4. A number of obstacles are strategically placed throughout a firefighter training maze. [Invert the sentence.]

Hacker/Sommers, *Exercises for A Canadian Writer's Reference*, 5th ed. (Boston: Bedford, 2012)

S7-1 | Sentence variety **17**

5. Ian McKellen is a British actor who made his debut in 1961 and was knighted in 1991, and he played Gandalf in the movie trilogy *The Lord of the Rings*. [Make a simple sentence. See also B4-a.]

Hacker/Sommers, *Exercises for A Canadian Writer's Reference*, 5th ed. (Boston: Bedford, 2012)

EXERCISE S7-2 ◆ Sentence variety

Before working this exercise, read section S7 in *A Canadian Writer's Reference*, Fifth Edition.

Edit the following paragraph to increase sentence variety.

Making architectural models is a skill that requires patience and precision. It is an art that illuminates a design. Architects come up with a grand and intricate vision. Draftspersons convert that vision into blueprints. The model maker follows the blueprints. The model maker builds a miniature version of the structure. Modellers can work in traditional materials like wood and clay and paint. Modellers can work in newer materials like Styrofoam and liquid polymers. Some modellers still use cardboard, paper, and glue. Other modellers prefer glue guns, deformable plastic, and thin aluminum and brass wire. The modeller may seem to be making a small mess in the early stages of model building. In the end the modeller has completed a small-scale structure. Architect Rem Koolhaas has insisted that plans reveal the logic of a design. He has argued that models expose the architect's vision. The model maker's art makes this vision real.

Hacker/Sommers, *Exercises for A Canadian Writer's Reference*, 5th ed. (Boston: Bedford, 2012)

S7-2 | Sentence variety **19**

EXERCISE W1-1 ◆ Usage

Before working this exercise, see the glossary of usage, section W1, in *A Canadian Writer's Reference*, Fifth Edition.

Edit the following sentences for problems in usage. If a sentence is correct, write "correct" after it. Revisions of lettered sentences appear in the back of the booklet. Example:

> *an*
> **The pediatrician gave my daughter ⌃a injection for her allergy.**

a. The amount of gifts a Nootka chief gave at a potlatch indicated his prestige in his tribe.

b. The cat just set there watching his prey.

c. The schoolchildren loved their new principal.

d. What is the capital of Brazil?

e. Chris redesigned the boundary plantings to try and improve the garden's overall design.

1. Will you except the offer?

2. Please phone for an hotel reservation at the Hotel Godin in Montreal.

3. Gary decided to buy more fruit and less snacks.

4. I usually shop first at the French Market, which is further away, and then stop at Food Mart on my way home.

5. Alan had been lying on the sidewalk unconscious for nearly two hours before help arrived.

Hacker/Sommers, *Exercises for A Canadian Writer's Reference*, 5th ed. (Boston: Bedford, 2012)

EXERCISE W2-1 ◆ Wordy sentences

Before working this exercise, read section W2 in *A Canadian Writer's Reference*, Fifth Edition.

Edit the following sentences to reduce wordiness. Revisions of lettered sentences appear in the back of the booklet. Example:

> *even though*
> The Wilsons moved into the house ~~in spite of the fact that~~ the back door was only
>   ^
> ten metres from the train tracks.

a. Martin Luther King Jr. was a man who set a high standard for future leaders to meet.

b. Alice has been deeply in love with cooking since she was little and could first peek over the edge of a big kitchen tabletop.

c. In my opinion, Bloom's race for the premiership is a futile exercise.

d. It is pretty important in being a successful graphic designer to have technical knowledge and at the same time an eye for colour and balance.

e. Your task will be the delivery of correspondence to all employees in the company.

1. Seeing the barrels, the driver immediately slammed on his brakes.

2. A really well-stocked bookshelf should have classical literature on it as well as important modern works of the current day.

3. China's enormously huge workforce has an effect on the global world of high-tech manufacturing of things.

4. A typical autocross course consists of at least two straightaways, and the rest of the course is made up of numerous slaloms and several sharp turns.

5. At breakfast time, Mehrdad always started his day with cantaloupe, lemon yogurt, and black coffee.

Hacker/Sommers, *Exercises for A Canadian Writer's Reference*, 5th ed. (Boston: Bedford, 2012)

W2-1 | Wordy sentences   21

EXERCISE W2-2 ◆ Wordy sentences

Before working this exercise, read section W2 in *A Canadian Writer's Reference*, Fifth Edition.

Edit the following business memo to reduce wordiness.

To: District managers

From: Margaret Davenport, Vice President

Subject: Customer database

It has recently been brought to my attention that a percentage of our sales representatives have been failing to log reports of their client calls in our customer database each and every day. I have also learned that some representatives are not checking the database on a routine basis.

Our clients sometimes receive a multiple number of sales calls from us when a sales representative is not cognizant of the fact that the client has been contacted at a previous time. Repeated telephone calls from our representatives annoy our customers. These repeated telephone calls also portray our company as one that is lacking in organization.

Effective as of immediately, direct your representatives to do the following:

- Record each and every customer contact in the customer database at the end of each day, without fail.
- Check the database at the very beginning of each day to ensure that telephone communications will not be initiated with clients who have already been called.

Let me extend my appreciation to you for cooperating in this important matter.

Hacker/Sommers, *Exercises for A Canadian Writer's Reference*, 5th ed. (Boston: Bedford, 2012)

EXERCISE W3-1 ◆ Active verbs

Before working this exercise, read section W3 in *A Canadian Writer's Reference*, Fifth Edition.

Revise any weak, unemphatic sentences by replacing *be* verbs or passive verbs with active alternatives. In some sentences, you may need to provide a subject that names the person or thing doing the action. If a sentence is already emphatic, do not change it. Revisions of lettered sentences appear in the back of the booklet. Example:

> *The warden doused the campfire before giving us*
> ~~The campfire was doused by the warden before we were given~~ a ticket for unauthorized
> ^
>
> use of a campsite.

a.   The Prussians were victorious over the Saxons in 1745.

b.   The entire operation is managed by Ahmed, the producer.

c.   The sea kayaks were expertly paddled by the tour guides.

d.   At the crack of rocket and mortar blasts, I jumped from the top bunk and landed on my buddy below, who was crawling on the floor looking for his boots.

e.   There were shouting protesters on the courthouse steps.

1.   A strange sound was made in the willow tree by the monkey that had escaped from the zoo.

2.   Her letter was in acknowledgment of the student's participation in the literacy program.

3.   The bomb bay doors rumbled open, and freezing air whipped through the plane.

4.   The work of Gordon Lightfoot and Leonard Cohen was influential in my choice of music for my audition.

5.   The only responsibility I was given by my parents was putting my little brother to bed when they had to work late.

EXERCISE W4-1 ◆ Jargon and pretentious language

Before working this exercise, read sections W4-a and W4-b in *A Canadian Writer's Reference*, Fifth Edition.

Edit the following sentences to eliminate jargon, pretentious or flowery language, euphemisms, and doublespeak. You may need to make substantial changes in some sentences. Revisions of lettered sentences appear in the back of the booklet. Example:

> *mastered*   *office*
> After two weeks in the legal department, Sue has ~~worked into~~ the routine, ~~of the office,~~
> *performance has*
> and her ~~functional and self-management skills have~~ exceeded all expectations.

a. In my youth, my family was under the constraints of difficult financial circumstances.

b. In order that I may increase my expertise in the area of delivery of services to clients, I feel that participation in this conference will be beneficial.

c. The prophetic meteorologist cautioned the general populace regarding the possible deleterious effects of the impending tempest.

d. Government-sanctioned investigations into the continued value of after-school programs indicate a perceived need in the public realm at large.

e. Passengers should endeavour to finalize the customs declaration form prior to exiting the aircraft.

1. We learned that the mayor had been engaging in a creative transfer of city employees' pension funds.

2. After a cursory examination of brand-new research findings on textiles, Patricia and the members of her team made the decision to engage in a series of visits to fashion manufacturers in the local vicinity.

3. The nurse announced that there had been a negative patient-care outcome due to a therapeutic misadventure on the part of the surgeon.

4. A generally leisurely pace at the onset of tai chi exercises can yield a variety of beneficial points within a short period of time.

5. The bottom line is that the company is experiencing a negative cash flow.

Hacker/Sommers, *Exercises for A Canadian Writer's Reference*, 5th ed. (Boston: Bedford, 2012)

EXERCISE W4-2 ◆ Slang and level of formality

Before working this exercise, read sections W4-c and W4-d in *A Canadian Writer's Reference*, Fifth Edition.

Revise the following passage so that the level of formality is appropriate for a letter to the editor of a major newspaper.

     In pop culture, university grads who return home to live with the folks are seen as good-for-nothing losers who mooch off their families. And many older adults seem to feel that the trend of moving back home after school, which was rare in their day, is becoming too commonplace today. But society must realize that times have changed. Most young adults want to live on their own ASAP, but they graduate with heaps of debt and need some time to get back on their feet. University tuition and the cost of housing have increased way more than salary increases in the past fifty years. Also, the job market is tighter and more jobs require advanced degrees than in the past. So before people go off on university graduates who move back into their parents' house for a spell, they'd better consider all the facts.

Hacker/Sommers, *Exercises for A Canadian Writer's Reference*, 5th ed. (Boston: Bedford, 2012)

W4-2 | Slang and level of formality   **25**

EXERCISE W4-3 ◆ Nonsexist language

Before working this exercise, read section W4-e in *A Canadian Writer's Reference*, Fifth Edition.

Edit the following sentences to eliminate sexist language or sexist assumptions. Revisions of lettered sentences appear in the back of the booklet. Example:

> *Scholarship athletes*   *their*   *they are*
> A scholarship athlete must be as concerned about ~~his~~ academic performance as ~~he is~~
>
>   *their*
> about ~~his~~ athletic performance.

a. Mrs. Geralyn Farmer, who is the mayor's wife, is the chief surgeon at University Hospital. Dr. Paul Green is her assistant.

b. Every applicant wants to know how much he will earn.

c. An elementary school teacher should understand the concept of nurturing if she intends to be effective.

d. An obstetrician needs to be available to his patients at all hours.

e. If man does not stop abusing natural resources and polluting his environment, mankind will perish.

1. A fireman must always be on call, even when he is off duty.

2. The chairman for the groundbreaking program in digital art is Ariana Tamlin, an accomplished portrait painter, computer programmer, and cookie baker.

3. In the mayor's race, Lena Weiss, a defence lawyer and mother of two, easily defeated Harvey Tower, an architect.

4. Recent military history has shown that lady combat helicopter pilots are as skilled, reliable, and resourceful as men.

5. An emergency room head nurse must know how to use sophisticated digital equipment if she is to keep track of all her patients' data and guide her medical team.

Hacker/Sommers, *Exercises for A Canadian Writer's Reference*, 5th ed. (Boston: Bedford, 2012)

EXERCISE W4-4 ◆ Nonsexist language

Before working this exercise, read section W4-e in *A Canadian Writer's Reference*, Fifth Edition.

Eliminate sexist language or sexist assumptions in the following job posting for an elementary school teacher.

We are looking for qualified women for the position of elementary school teacher. The ideal candidate should have a bachelor's degree, a teaching certificate, and one year of student teaching. She should be knowledgeable in all elementary subject areas, including science and math. While we want our new teacher to have a commanding presence in the classroom, we are also looking for motherly characteristics such as patience and trustworthiness. She must be able to both motivate an entire classroom and work with each student one-on-one to assess his individual needs. She must also be comfortable communicating with the parents of her students. For salary and benefits information, including maternity leave policy, please contact the Upper Canada District School Board. Any qualified applicant should submit her résumé by March 15.

Hacker/Sommers, *Exercises for A Canadian Writer's Reference*, 5th ed. (Boston: Bedford, 2012)

W4-4 | Nonsexist language **27**

EXERCISE W5-1 ◆ Synonyms

Before working this exercise, read section W5-a in *A Canadian Writer's Reference*, Fifth Edition.

Use a dictionary and a thesaurus to find at least four synonyms for each of the following words. Be prepared to explain any slight differences in meaning.

1.   decay (verb)

2.   difficult (adjective)

3.   hurry (verb)

4.   pleasure (noun)

5.   secret (adjective)

6.   talent (noun)

Hacker/Sommers, *Exercises for A Canadian Writer's Reference*, 5th ed. (Boston: Bedford, 2012)

EXERCISE W5-2 ◆ Misused words

Before working this exercise, read section W5-c in *A Canadian Writer's Reference*, Fifth Edition.

Edit the following sentences to correct misused words. Revisions of lettered sentences appear in the back of the booklet. Example:

> *all-absorbing.*
> **These days the training required for a ballet dancer is** ~~all-absorbent.~~
>   ∧

a.   We regret this delay; thank you for your patients.

b.   Ada's plan is to require education and experience to prepare herself for a position as property manager.

c.   Roger Federer, the penultimate competitor, has earned millions of dollars just in endorsements.

d.   Many people take for granite that public libraries have up-to-date computer systems.

e.   The affect of Gao Xinjian's novels on Chinese exiles is hard to gauge.

1.   Because Anne Tyler often writes about family loyalties, her illusions to *King Lear* are not surprising.

2.   Designers of handheld devices understand that changes in ambience temperatures can damage the tiny circuit boards.

3.   The Keweenaw Peninsula is surrounded on three sides by Lake Superior.

4.   At the cooking school in Tuscany, I learned that rosemary is a perfect compliment to lamb.

5.   The person who complained to the human resources manager wants to remain unanimous.

EXERCISE W5-3 ◆ Standard idioms

Before working this exercise, read section W5-d in *A Canadian Writer's Reference*, Fifth Edition.

Edit the following sentences to eliminate errors in the use of idiomatic expressions. If a sentence is correct, write "correct" after it. Answers to lettered sentences appear in the back of the booklet. Example:

> by
> We agreed to abide ~~with~~ the decision of the judge.
> ^

a. Queen Anne was so angry at Sarah Churchill that she refused to see her again.

b. Jean-Pierre's ambitious travel plans made it impossible for him to comply with the residency requirement for the graduate program.

c. The parade moved off of the street and onto the beach.

d. The frightened refugees intend on making the dangerous trek across the mountains.

e. What type of a wedding are you planning?

1. Be sure and report on the danger of releasing genetically engineered bacteria into the atmosphere.

2. Why do you assume that embezzling bank assets is so different than robbing the bank?

3. The wilderness guide seemed capable to show us where the trail of petroglyphs was located.

4. In Evan's cautious mind, packing his own parachute seemed preferable to letting an indifferent teenager fold all that silk and cord into a small pack.

5. Andrea plans on joining the Peace Corps after graduation.

Hacker/Sommers, *Exercises for A Canadian Writer's Reference,* 5th ed. (Boston: Bedford, 2012)

EXERCISE W5-4 ◆ Clichés and mixed figures of speech

Before working this exercise, read sections W5-e and W5-f in *A Canadian Writer's Reference*, Fifth Edition.

Edit the following sentences to replace worn-out expressions and clarify mixed figures of speech. Revisions of lettered sentences appear in the back of the booklet. Example:

> *the colour drained from his face.*
> **When he heard about the accident, ~~he turned white as a sheet.~~**
> ^

a.   John stormed into the room like a bull in a china shop.

b.   Some people insist that they'll always be there for you, even when they haven't been before.

c.   The Blue Jays easily beat the Mets, who were in the soup early in the game today at the

     Rogers Centre.

d.   We ironed out the sticky spots in our relationship.

e.   My mother accused me of beating around the bush when in fact I was just talking off the top

     of my head.

1.   Priscilla was used to burning the candle at both ends to get her assignments done.

2.   No matter how many books he reads, André can never seem to quench his thirst for

     knowledge.

3.   In an era of cutbacks and outsourcing, the best tech-savvy workers discover that being a

     jack of all trades is a solid gold key to continued success.

4.   Too many cooks are spoiling the broth at corporate headquarters.

5.   Juanita told Kyle that keeping skeletons in the closet would be playing with fire.

EXERCISE G1-1 ◆ Subject-verb agreement

Before working this exercise, read section G1 in *A Canadian Writer's Reference*, Fifth Edition.

For each sentence in the following passage, underline the subject (or compound subject) and then select the verb that agrees with it. (If you have trouble identifying the subject, consult B2-a.)

Loggerhead sea turtles (migrate / migrates) thousands of kilometres before returning to their nesting location every two to three years. The nesting season for loggerhead turtles (span / spans) the hottest months of the summer. Although the habitat of Atlantic loggerheads (range / ranges) from Newfoundland to Argentina, nesting for these turtles (take / takes) place primarily along the southeastern coast of the United States. Female turtles that have reached sexual maturity (crawl / crawls) ashore at night to lay their eggs. The cavity that serves as a nest for the eggs (is / are) dug out with the female's strong flippers. Deposited into each nest (is / are) anywhere from fifty to two hundred spherical eggs, also known as a *clutch*. After a two-month incubation period, all eggs in the clutch (begin / begins) to hatch, and within a few days the young turtles attempt to make their way into the ocean. A major cause of the loggerhead's decreasing numbers (is / are) natural predators such as raccoons, birds, and crabs. Beach erosion and coastal development also (threaten / threatens) the turtles' survival. For example, a crowd of curious humans or lights from beachfront residences (is / are) enough to make the female abandon her nesting plans and return to the ocean. Since only one in one thousand loggerheads survives to adulthood, special care should be taken to protect this threatened species.

Hacker/Sommers, *Exercises for A Canadian Writer's Reference*, 5th ed. (Boston: Bedford, 2012)

EXERCISE G1-2 ◆ Subject-verb agreement

Before working this exercise, read section G1 in *A Canadian Writer's Reference*, Fifth Edition.

Edit the following sentences to eliminate problems with subject-verb agreement. If a sentence is correct, write "correct" after it. Answers to lettered sentences appear in the back of the booklet. Example:

were

Jack's first days in the infantry ~~was~~ gruelling.
^

a. One of the main reasons for elephant poaching are the profits received from selling the ivory tusks.

b. Not until my interview with Dr. Han were other possibilities opened to me.

c. A number of students in the seminar was aware of the importance of joining the discussion.

d. Batik cloth from Bali, blue and white ceramics from Delft, and a bocce ball from Turin has made Angelie's room the talk of the dorm.

e. The board of directors, ignoring the wishes of the neighbourhood, has voted to allow further development.

1. Measles is a contagious childhood disease.

2. Adorning a shelf in the lab is a Vietnamese figurine, a set of Korean clay gods, and a plastic maple leaf.

3. The presence of certain bacteria in our bodies is one of the factors that determines our overall health.

4. Sheila is the only one of the many applicants who has the ability to step into this job.

5. Neither the explorer nor his companions was ever seen again.

EXERCISE G2-1 ◆ Irregular verbs

Before working this exercise, read section G2-a in *A Canadian Writer's Reference*, Fifth Edition.

Edit the following sentences to eliminate problems with irregular verbs. If a sentence is correct, write "correct" after it. Answers to lettered sentences appear in the back of the booklet. Example:

> *saw*
> **The warden ~~seen~~ the forest fire fifteen kilometres away.**
> ^

a. When I get the urge to exercise, I lay down until it passes.

b. Grandmother had drove our new SUV to the sunrise church service on Savage Mountain, so we were left with the station wagon.

c. A pile of dirty rags was laying at the bottom of the stairs.

d. How did the computer know that the gamer had went from the room with the blue ogre to the hall where the gold was heaped?

e. The computer programmer was an expert in online security; he was confident that the encryption code he used could never be broke.

1. The burglar must have gone immediately upstairs, grabbed what looked good, and took off.

2. Have you ever dreamed that you were falling from a cliff or flying through the air?

3. Tomás reached for the pen, signed the title page of his novel, and then laid the book on the table for the first customer in line.

4. In her junior year, Cindy run the 400-metre dash in 51.1 seconds.

5. Larry claimed that he had drank too much pop, but Esther suspected the truth.

Hacker/Sommers, *Exercises for A Canadian Writer's Reference*, 5th ed. (Boston: Bedford, 2012)

EXERCISE G2-2 ◆ -s and -ed verb endings and omitted verbs

Before working this exercise, read sections G2-c to G2-e in *A Canadian Writer's Reference*, Fifth Edition.

Edit the following sentences to eliminate problems with -s and -ed verb forms and with omitted verbs. If a sentence is correct, write "correct" after it. Answers to lettered sentences appear in the back of the booklet. Example:

covers

The SSHRC Doctoral Fellowship sometimes ~~cover~~ the student's full tuition.
^

a. The glass sculptures of the Swan Boats was prominent in the brightly lit lobby.

b. Visitors to the glass museum were not suppose to touch the delicate exhibits.

c. Our church has all the latest technology, even a close-circuit television.

d. Christos didn't know about Marlo's promotion because he never listens. He always talking.

e. Most psychologists agree that no one performs well under stress.

1. Have there ever been a time in your life when you were too depressed to get out of bed?

2. My days in this department have taught me to do what I'm told without asking questions.

3. We have change our plan and are waiting out the storm before packing the truck.

4. Winter training for search-and-rescue divers consist of building up a tolerance to icy water temperatures.

5. How would you feel if a love one had been a victim of a crime like this?

EXERCISE G2-3 ◆ Verb tense and mood

Before working this exercise, read sections G2-f and G2-g in *A Canadian Writer's Reference*, Fifth Edition.

Edit the following sentences to eliminate errors in verb tense or mood. If a sentence is correct, write "correct" after it. Answers to lettered sentences appear in the back of the booklet. Example:

> *had been*
> **After the path ~~was~~ plowed, we were able to walk through the park.**
>   ^

a. The palace of Knossos in Crete is believed to have been destroyed by fire around 1375 BCE.

b. Watson and Crick discovered the mechanism that controlled inheritance in all life: the workings of the DNA molecule.

c. When city planners proposed rezoning the waterfront, did they know that the mayor promised to curb development in that neighbourhood?

d. Tonight's concert begins at 9:30. If it were earlier, I'd consider going.

e. As soon as my aunt applied for the position of pastor, the post was filled by an inexperienced seminary graduate who had been so hastily snatched that his mortarboard was still in midair.

1. Don Quixote, in Cervantes's novel, was an idealist ill suited for life in the real world.

2. Visiting the technology museum inspired the high school seniors and had reminded them that science can be fun.

3. I would like to have been on the *Stakesby* but not to have experienced the first winter.

4. When the director yelled "Action!" I forgot my lines, even though I practised my part every waking hour for three days.

5. If midday naps were a regular practice in Canadian workplaces, employees would be far more productive.

Hacker/Sommers, *Exercises for A Canadian Writer's Reference*, 5th ed. (Boston: Bedford, 2012)

EXERCISE G3-1 ◆ Pronoun-antecedent agreement

Before working this exercise, read section G3-a in *A Canadian Writer's Reference*, Fifth Edition.

Edit the following sentences to eliminate problems with pronoun-antecedent agreement. Most of the sentences can be revised in more than one way, so experiment before choosing a solution. If a sentence is correct, write "correct" after it. Revisions of lettered sentences appear in the back of the booklet. Example:

> *Recruiters*
> ~~The recruiter~~ may tell the truth, but there is much that they choose not to tell.
> ^

a. Every candidate for prime minister must appeal to a wide variety of ethnic and social groups if they want to win the election.

b. David lent his motorcycle to someone who allowed their friend to use it.

c. The aerobics teacher motioned for everyone to move their arms in wide, slow circles.

d. The parade committee was unanimous in its decision to allow all groups and organizations to join the festivities.

e. The applicant should be bilingual if they want to qualify for this position.

1. If a driver refuses to take a blood or breath test, he or she will have their licences suspended for six months.

2. Why should anyone learn a second language? One reason is to sharpen their minds.

3. The Ministry of Education issued guidelines for school security. They were trying to anticipate problems and avert disaster.

4. The logger in the Northwest relies on the old-growth forest for their living.

5. If anyone notices any suspicious activity, they should report it to the police.

Hacker/Sommers, *Exercises for A Canadian Writer's Reference*, 5th ed. (Boston: Bedford, 2012)

G3-1 | Pronoun-antecedent agreement **37**

EXERCISE G3-2 ◆ Pronoun-antecedent agreement

Before working this exercise, read section G3-a in *A Canadian Writer's Reference*, Fifth Edition.

Edit the following paragraph to eliminate problems with pronoun-antecedent agreement or sexist language.

A common practice in businesses is to put each employee in their own cubicle. A typical cubicle resembles an office, but their walls don't reach the ceiling. Many office managers feel that a cubicle floor plan has its advantages. Cubicles make a large area feel spacious. In addition, they can be moved around so that each new employee can be accommodated in his own work area. Of course, the cubicle model also has problems. The typical employee is not as happy with a cubicle as they would be with a traditional office. Also, productivity can suffer. Neither a manager nor a frontline worker can ordinarily do their best work in a cubicle because of noise and lack of privacy. Each worker can hear his neighbours tapping on computer keyboards, making telephone calls, and muttering under their breath.

Hacker/Sommers, *Exercises for A Canadian Writer's Reference*, 5th ed. (Boston: Bedford, 2012)

EXERCISE G3-3 ◆ Pronoun reference

Before working this exercise, read section G3-b in *A Canadian Writer's Reference*, Fifth Edition.

Edit the following sentences to correct errors in pronoun reference. In some cases, you will need to decide on an antecedent that the pronoun might logically refer to. Revisions of lettered sentences appear in the back of the booklet. Example:

> **Although Apple makes the most widely recognized MP3 player, other companies have**
> *The competition*
> **gained a share of the market.** ~~**This**~~ **has kept prices from skyrocketing.**
> ^

a. They say that engineering students should have hands-on experience with dismantling and reassembling machines.

b. She had decorated her living room with posters from chamber music festivals. This led her date to believe that she was interested in classical music. Actually she preferred rock.

c. In my high school, you didn't need to get all A's to be considered a success; you just needed to work to your ability.

d. Marianne told Jenny that she was worried about her mother's illness.

e. Though Lewis cried for several minutes after scraping his knee, eventually it subsided.

1. I've decided to be a business major. It will give me plenty of options.

2. Many people believe that the polygraph test is highly reliable if you employ a licensed examiner.

3. Parent involvement is high at Miramichi Valley High School. They participate in many committees and activities that affect all aspects of school life.

4. Because of Paul Robeson's outspoken attitude toward fascism, he was labelled a Communist.

5. In the report, it points out that the trumpeter swan, after several decades of protection, was removed from the endangered species list in Canada in 1996.

EXERCISE G3-4 ◆ Pronoun reference

Before working this exercise, read section G3-b in *A Canadian Writer's Reference*, Fifth Edition.

Edit the following passage to correct errors in pronoun reference. In some cases, you will need to decide on an antecedent that the pronoun might logically refer to.

Since the Internet's inception in the 1980s, it has grown to be one of the world's largest forums for communication. The Internet was created by a team of academics who were building on a platform that government scientists had started developing in the 1950s. They initially viewed it as a noncommercial enterprise that would serve only the needs of the academic and technical communities. But with the introduction of user-friendly browser technology in the 1990s, it expanded tremendously. By the late 1990s, many businesses were connecting to the Internet with high-speed broadband and fibre-optic connections, which is also true of many home users today. Accessing information, shopping, and communicating are easier than ever before. This, however, can lead to some possible downfalls. You can be bombarded with spam and pop-up ads or attacked by harmful viruses and worms. They say that the best way to protect home computers from harm is to keep antivirus protection programs up-to-date and to shut them down when not in use.

Hacker/Sommers, *Exercises for A Canadian Writer's Reference*, 5th ed. (Boston: Bedford, 2012)

EXERCISE G3-5 ◆ Pronoun case: personal pronouns

Before working this exercise, read section G3-c in *A Canadian Writer's Reference*, Fifth Edition.

Edit the following sentences to eliminate errors in pronoun case. If a sentence is correct, write "correct" after it. Answers to lettered sentences appear in the back of the booklet. Example:

> *he.*
> **Grandfather cuts down trees for neighbours much younger than ~~him.~~**
> ^

a. Rick applied for the job even though he heard that other candidates were more experienced than he.

b. The volleyball team could not believe that the coach was she.

c. She appreciated him telling the truth in such a difficult situation.

d. The director has asked you and I to draft a proposal for a new recycling plan.

e. Five close friends and myself rented a van, packed it with food, and drove two hundred kilometres to the Calgary Stampede.

1. The squawk of the brass horns nearly overwhelmed us oboe and bassoon players.

2. Ushio, the last rock climber up the wall, tossed Teri and she the remaining pitons and carabiners.

3. The programmer realized that her and the interface designers were creating an entirely new Web application.

4. My desire to understand classical music was aided by me working as an usher at Symphony Hall.

5. The shower of sinking bricks caused he and his diving partner to race away from the collapsing seawall.

Hacker/Sommers, *Exercises for A Canadian Writer's Reference*, 5th ed. (Boston: Bedford, 2012)

G3-5 | Pronoun case: personal pronouns   **41**

EXERCISE G3-6 ◆ Pronoun case

Before working this exercise, read section G3-c in *A Canadian Writer's Reference*, Fifth Edition.

In the following paragraph, choose the correct pronoun in each set of parentheses.

We may blame television for the number of products based on characters in children's TV shows—from Big Bird to SpongeBob—but in fact merchandising that capitalizes on a character's popularity started long before television. Raggedy Ann began as a child's rag doll, and a few years later books about (she / her) and her brother, Raggedy Andy, were published. A cartoonist named Johnny Gruelle painted a cloth face on a family doll and applied for a patent in 1915. Later Gruelle began writing and illustrating stories about Raggedy Ann, and in 1918 (he / him) and a publisher teamed up to publish the books and sell the dolls. He was not the only one to try to sell products linked to children's stories. Beatrix Potter published the first of many Peter Rabbit picture books in 1902, and no one was better than (she / her) at making a living from spin-offs. After Peter Rabbit and Benjamin Bunny became popular, Potter began putting pictures of (they / them) and their little animal friends on merchandise. Potter had fans all over the world, and she understood (them / their) wanting to see Peter Rabbit not only in books but also on teapots and plates and lamps and other furnishings for the nursery. Potter and Gruelle, like countless others before and since, knew that entertaining children could be a profitable business.

Hacker/Sommers, *Exercises for A Canadian Writer's Reference*, 5th ed. (Boston: Bedford, 2012)

EXERCISE G3-7 ◆ Pronoun case: *who* and *whom*

Before working this exercise, read section G3-d in *A Canadian Writer's Reference*, Fifth Edition.

Edit the following sentences to eliminate errors in the use of *who* and *whom* (or *whoever* and *whomever*). If a sentence is correct, write "correct" after it. Answers to lettered sentences appear in the back of the booklet. Example:

> *whom*
> **What is the address of the artist ~~who~~ Antonio hired?**
> ^

a. The roundtable featured scholars who I had never heard of.

b. Arriving late for rehearsal, we had no idea who was supposed to dance with whom.

c. Whom did you support for student government president?

d. Daniel always gives a holiday donation to whomever needs it.

e. So many singers came to the audition that Natalia had trouble deciding who to select for the choir.

1. My cousin Sylvie, who I am teaching to fly a kite, watches us every time we compete.

2. Who decided to research the history of Hungarians in New Brunswick?

3. According to the Greek myth, the Sphinx devoured those who could not answer her riddles.

4. The people who ordered their medications from Canada were retirees whom don't have health insurance.

5. Who did the committee select?

Hacker/Sommers, *Exercises for A Canadian Writer's Reference*, 5th ed. (Boston: Bedford, 2012)

G3-7 | Pronoun case: *who* and *whom*   **43**

EXERCISE G4-1 ◆ Adjectives and adverbs

Before working this exercise, read section G4 in *A Canadian Writer's Reference*, Fifth Edition.

Edit the following sentences to eliminate errors in the use of adjectives and adverbs. If a sentence is correct, write "correct" after it. Answers to lettered sentences appear in the back of the booklet. Example:

>   *well*
> **We weren't surprised by how ~~good~~ the sidecar racing team flowed through the**
>   ^
> **tricky course.**

a. Did you do good on last week's chemistry exam?

b. With the budget deadline approaching, our office hasn't hardly had time to handle routine correspondence.

c. Some flowers smell surprisingly bad.

d. The customer complained that he hadn't been treated nice.

e. Of all my relatives, Uncle Roberto is the most cleverest.

1. When you answer the phone, speak clear and courteous.

2. Who was more upset about the loss? Was it the coach or the quarterback or the owner of the team?

3. To a novice skateboarder, even the basic ollie seems real challenging.

4. After checking how bad I had been hurt, my sister dialled 911.

5. If the university's Web page had been updated more regular, students would have learned about the new course offerings.

Hacker/Sommers, *Exercises for A Canadian Writer's Reference*, 5th ed. (Boston: Bedford, 2012)

EXERCISE G4-2 ◆ Adjectives and adverbs

Before working this exercise, read section G4 in *A Canadian Writer's Reference*, Fifth Edition.

Edit the following passage to eliminate errors in the use of adjectives and adverbs.

Doctors recommend that to give skin the most fullest protection from ultraviolet rays, people should use plenty of sunscreen, limit sun exposure, and wear protective clothing. The commonest sunscreens today are known as "broad spectrum" because they block out both UVA and UVB rays. These lotions don't feel any differently on the skin from the old UVA-only types, but they work best at preventing premature aging and skin cancer. Many sunscreens claim to be waterproof, but they won't hardly provide adequate coverage after extended periods of swimming or perspiring. To protect good, even waterproof sunscreens should be reapplied liberal and often. All areas of exposed skin, including ears, backs of hands, and tops of feet, need to be coated good to avoid burning or damage. Some people's skin reacts bad to PABA, or para-aminobenzoic acid, so PABA-free (hypoallergenic) sunscreens are widely available. In addition to recommending sunscreen, doctors almost unanimously agree that people should stay out of the sun when rays are the most strongest—between 10:00 a.m. and 3:00 p.m.—and should limit time in the sun. They also suggest that people wear long-sleeved shirts, broad-brimmed hats, and long pants whenever possible.

EXERCISE G5-1 ◆ Sentence fragments

Before working this exercise, read section G5 in *A Canadian Writer's Reference*, Fifth Edition.

Repair any fragment by attaching it to a nearby sentence or by rewriting it as a complete sentence. If a word group is correct, write "correct" after it. Revisions of lettered sentences appear in the back of the booklet. Example:

> One Greek island that should not be missed is Mykonos/. A vacation spot for Europeans and a playground for the rich and famous.

a. Listening to the CD her sister had sent, Mia was overcome with a mix of emotions. Happiness, homesickness, and nostalgia.

b. Cortés and his soldiers were astonished when they looked down from the mountains and saw Tenochtitlán. The magnificent capital of the Aztec Empire.

c. Although my spoken French is not very good. I can read the language with ease.

d. There are several reasons for not eating meat. One reason being that dangerous chemicals are used throughout the various stages of meat production.

e. To learn how to sculpt beauty from everyday life. This is my intention in studying art and archaeology.

1. The cougar lay motionless behind the rock. Waiting silently for its prey.

2. Aunt Mina loved to play all my favourite games. Cat's cradle, Uno, mancala, and even four square.

3. With machetes, the explorers cut their way through the tall grasses to the edge of the canyon. Then they began to lay out the tapes for the survey.

4. The owners of the online grocery store rented a warehouse in the Market district. An area catering to small businesses.

5. If a woman from the desert tribe showed anger toward her husband, she was whipped in front of the whole village. And shunned by the rest of the women.

Hacker/Sommers, *Exercises for A Canadian Writer's Reference*, 5th ed. (Boston: Bedford, 2012)

EXERCISE G5-2 ◆ Sentence fragments

Before working this exercise, read section G5 in *A Canadian Writer's Reference*, Fifth Edition.

Repair each fragment in the following passage by attaching it to a sentence nearby or by rewriting it as a complete sentence.

Digital technology has revolutionized information delivery. Forever blurring the lines between information and entertainment. Yesterday's readers of books and newspapers are today's readers of e-books and news blogs. Countless readers have moved on from print information entirely. Choosing instead to point, click, and scroll their way through a text on their Amazon Kindle or in an online forum. Once a nation of people spoon-fed television commercials and the six o'clock evening news. We are now seemingly addicted to *YouTube*. Remember the family trip when Dad or Mom wrestled with a road map? On the way to Banff or Whistler? No wrestling is required with a slick GPS navigator by the driver's side. Unless it's Mom and Dad wrestling over who gets to program the address. Accessing information now seems to be our favourite pastime. Statistics Canada, in its Canadian Internet Use Survey, reports that 80 percent of Canadian adults use the Internet for personal reasons. Connecting mostly from home. As a country, we embrace information and communication technologies. Which include iPods, cell phones, laptops, and handheld devices. Among children and adolescents, Internet and other personal technology use is on the rise. For activities like socializing, gaming, and information gathering.

Hacker/Sommers, *Exercises for A Canadian Writer's Reference*, 5th ed. (Boston: Bedford, 2012)

G5-2 | Sentence fragments   **47**

EXERCISE G6-1 ◆ Run-on sentences

Before working this exercise, read section G6 in *A Canadian Writer's Reference*, Fifth Edition.

Revise the following run-on sentences by using the method of revision suggested in brackets. Revisions of lettered sentences appear in the back of the booklet. Example:

> *Because*
> **Orville had been obsessed with his weight as a teenager, he rarely ate anything**
> ^
> **sweet.** [Restructure the sentence.]

a. The city had one public swimming pool, it stayed packed with children all summer long. [Restructure the sentence.]

b. The building is being renovated, therefore at times we have no heat, water, or electricity. [Use a comma and a coordinating conjunction.]

c. The view was not what the travel agent had described, where were the rolling hills and the shimmering rivers? [Make two sentences.]

d. All those gnarled equations looked like toxic insects, maybe I was going to have to rethink my major. [Use a semicolon.]

e. City officials had good reason to fear a major earthquake, most of the business district was built on landfill. [Use a colon.]

1. The car was hardly worth trading, the frame was twisted and the block was warped. [Restructure the sentence.]

2. The next time an event is cancelled because of bad weather, don't blame the meteorologist, blame nature. [Make two sentences.]

3. Ray was fluent in American Sign Language he could sign as easily as he could speak. [Restructure the sentence.]

4. Susanna arrived with a stack of her latest hats she hoped the gift shop would place a big winter order. [Restructure the sentence.]

5. There was one major reason for John's wealth, his grandfather had been a multimillionaire. [Use a colon.]

Hacker/Sommers, *Exercises for A Canadian Writer's Reference*, 5th ed. (Boston: Bedford, 2012)

EXERCISE G6-2 ◆ Run-on sentences

Before working this exercise, read section G6 in *A Canadian Writer's Reference*, Fifth Edition.

Revise any run-on sentences using a technique that you find effective. If a sentence is correct, write "correct" after it. Revisions of lettered sentences appear in the back of the booklet. Example:

> **Crossing so many time zones on an eight-hour flight, I knew I would be tired when I**
>   *but*
> **arrived, ~~however,~~ I was too excited to sleep on the plane.**
>   ^

a. Wind power for the home is a supplementary source of energy, it can be combined with electricity, gas, or solar energy.

b. Aidan viewed Sofia Coppola's *Lost in Translation* three times and then wrote a paper describing the film as the work of a mysterious modern painter.

c. In the Middle Ages, the streets of London were dangerous places, it was safer to travel by boat along the Thames.

d. "He's not drunk," I said, "he's in a state of diabetic shock."

e. Are you able to endure extreme angle turns, high speeds, frequent jumps, and occasional crashes, then supermoto racing may be a sport for you.

1. Death Valley National Monument, located in southern California and Nevada, is one of the hottest places on earth, temperatures there have soared as high as 57 °C.

2. Anamaria opened the boxes crammed with toys, out sprang griffins, dragons, and phoenixes.

3. Subatomic physics is filled with strange and marvellous particles, tiny bodies of matter that shiver, wobble, pulse, and flatten to no thickness at all.

4. In the centre of Halifax are the Halifax Public Gardens, one of the finest examples in North America of formal Victorian gardens.

5. The neurosurgeon explained that the medication could have one side effect, it might cause me to experience temporary memory loss.

EXERCISE G6-3 ◆ Run-on sentences

Before working this exercise, read section G6 in *A Canadian Writer's Reference*, Fifth Edition.

In the following rough draft, revise any run-on sentences.

Some parents and educators argue that requiring uniforms in public schools would improve student behaviour and performance. They think that uniforms give students a more professional attitude toward school, moreover, they believe that uniforms help create a sense of community among students from diverse backgrounds. But parents and educators should consider the drawbacks to requiring uniforms in public schools.

Uniforms do create a sense of community, they do this, however, by stamping out individuality. Youth is a time to express originality, it is a time to develop a sense of self. One important way young people express their identities is through the clothes they wear. The self-patrolled dress code of high school students may be stricter than any school-imposed code, nevertheless, trying to control dress habits from above will only lead to resentment or to mindless conformity.

If children are going to act like adults, they need to be treated like adults, they need to be allowed to make their own choices. Telling young people what to wear to school merely prolongs their childhood. Requiring uniforms undermines the educational purpose of public schools, which is not just to teach facts and figures but to help young people grow into adults who are responsible for making their own choices.

Hacker/Sommers, *Exercises for A Canadian Writer's Reference*, 5th ed. (Boston: Bedford, 2012)

EXERCISE M1-1 ◆ Verb forms and tenses

Before working this exercise, read sections M1-a and M1-b in *A Canadian Writer's Reference*, Fifth Edition.

Revise the following sentences to correct errors in verb forms and tenses in the active and the passive voice. You may need to look at G2-a for the correct form of some irregular verbs and at G2-f for help with tenses. Answers to lettered sentences appear in the back of the booklet. Example:

> *begins*
> **The meeting ~~begin~~ tonight at 7:30.**
> ^

a. In the past, tobacco companies deny any connection between smoking and health problems.

b. There is nothing in the world that TV has not touch on.

c. I am wanting to register for a summer tutoring session.

d. By the end of the year, the province will have test 139 birds for avian flu.

e. The benefits of eating fruits and vegetables have been promoting by health care providers.

1. By the time he was twelve years old, Mozart had compose an entire opera.

2. The sound was occurred whenever someone stepped on the loose board.

3. My family has been gone to Sam's restaurant ever since we moved to this neighbourhood.

4. I have ate Thai food only once before.

5. The bear is appearing to be sedated.

Hacker/Sommers, *Exercises for A Canadian Writer's Reference*, 5th ed. (Boston: Bedford, 2012)

M1-1 | Verb forms and tenses   **51**

EXERCISE M1-2 ◆ Verb forms with modals

Before working this exercise, read section M1-c in *A Canadian Writer's Reference*, Fifth Edition.

Edit the following sentences to correct errors in the use of verb forms with modals. You may find it helpful to consult the chart on pages 232–33 in the handbook. If a sentence is correct, write "correct" after it. Answers to lettered sentences appear in the back of the booklet. Example:

We should ~~to~~ order pizza for dinner.

a. Many major league pitchers can to throw a baseball over ninety-five miles per hour.

b. The writing centre tutor will helps you revise your essay.

c. A reptile must adjusted its body temperature to its environment.

d. In some provinces, individuals may renew a driver's licence online or in person.

e. My uncle, a cartoonist, could sketched a person's face in less than two minutes.

1. Working more than twelve hours a day might to contribute to insomnia, according to researchers.

2. A wasp will carry its immobilized prey back to the nest.

3. Hikers should to carry plenty of water on a hot day.

4. Should we continued to submit hard copies of our essays?

5. Physical therapy may helps people after heart surgery.

Hacker/Sommers, *Exercises for A Canadian Writer's Reference*, 5th ed. (Boston: Bedford, 2012)

EXERCISE M1-3 ◆ Negative verb forms and conditional verbs

Before working this exercise, read sections M1-d and M1-e in *A Canadian Writer's Reference*, Fifth Edition.

Edit the following sentences to correct problems with negative verb forms and conditional verbs. In some cases, more than one revision is possible. Suggested revisions of lettered sentences appear in the back of the booklet. Example:

> *had*
> **If I ~~have~~ time, I would study both French and Russian next semester.**
> ^

a. The electrician might have discovered the broken circuit if she went through the modules one at a time.

b. If Verena goes to the meeting, she would be late for work.

c. Whenever there is a fire in our neighbourhood, everybody came out to watch.

d. Sarah did not understood the terms of her internship.

e. If I live in Budapest with my cousin Szusza, she would teach me Hungarian cooking.

1. If the science fiction festival starts Monday, we wouldn't need to plan entertainment for our visitors.

2. If everyone has voted in the last election, the results would have been very different.

3. The tenants will not pay the rent unless the landlord fixed the furnace.

4. When dark grey clouds appeared on a hot summer afternoon, a thunderstorm often follows.

5. Rosalie should no offer to volunteer on school nights.

EXERCISE M1-4 ◆ Verbs followed by gerunds or infinitives

Before working this exercise, read section M1-f in *A Canadian Writer's Reference*, Fifth Edition.

Form sentences by adding gerund or infinitive constructions to the following sentence openings. In some cases, more than one kind of construction is possible. Possible sentences for lettered items appear in the back of the booklet. Example:

> **Please remind** *your sister to call me.*
> ^

a. I enjoy

b. The tutor told Samantha

c. The team hopes

d. Ricardo and his brothers miss

e. The babysitter let

1. Pollen makes

2. The club president asked

3. Next summer we plan

4. My supervisor intends

5. Please stop

Hacker/Sommers, *Exercises for A Canadian Writer's Reference*, 5th ed. (Boston: Bedford, 2012)

EXERCISE M2-1 ◆ Articles and types of nouns

Before working this exercise, read section M2 in *A Canadian Writer's Reference*, Fifth Edition.

Edit the following sentences for proper use of articles and nouns. If a sentence is correct, write "correct" after it. Answers to lettered sentences appear in the back of the booklet. Example:

> ~~The~~ Josefina's dance routine was flawless.

a. Doing volunteer work often brings a satisfaction.

b. As I looked out the window of the plane, I could see the Lions Bay.

c. Melina likes to drink her coffees with lots of cream.

d. Recovering from abdominal surgery requires patience.

e. I completed the my homework assignment quickly.

1. The lawyer argued that her client should receive a money for emotional suffering.

2. Please check to see if there is a mail in the mailbox.

3. The Pier 21 is known for its photographic archive and other immigration-related artifacts.

4. A cement is one of the components in concrete.

5. I took all the boys on the roller coaster after lunch.

EXERCISE M2-2 ◆ Articles

Before working this exercise, read section M2 in *A Canadian Writer's Reference*, Fifth Edition.

Articles have been omitted from the following description of winter weather. Insert the articles *a*, *an*, and *the* where English requires them and be prepared to explain the reasons for your choices.

Many people confuse terms *hail*, *sleet*, and *freezing rain*. Hail normally occurs in thunderstorm and is caused by strong updrafts that lift growing chunks of ice into clouds. When chunks of ice, called hailstones, become too heavy to be carried by updrafts, they fall to ground. Hailstones can cause damage to crops, windshields, and people. Sleet occurs during winter storms and is caused by snowflakes falling from layer of cold air into warm layer, where they become raindrops, and then into another cold layer. As they fall through last layer of cold air, raindrops freeze and become small ice pellets, forming sleet. When it hits car windshield or windows of house, sleet can make annoying racket. Driving and walking can be hazardous when sleet accumulates on roads and sidewalks. Freezing rain is basically rain that falls onto ground and then freezes after it hits ground. It causes icy glaze on trees and any surface that is below freezing.

Hacker/Sommers, *Exercises for A Canadian Writer's Reference*, 5th ed. (Boston: Bedford, 2012)

EXERCISE M3-1 ◆ Omissions and repetitions

Before working this exercise, read sections M3-a to M3-d in *A Canadian Writer's Reference*, Fifth Edition.

In the following sentences, add needed subjects or expletives (placeholders) and delete any repeated subjects, objects, or adverbs. Answers to lettered sentences appear in the back of the booklet. Example:

> **The new geology professor is the one we saw ~~him~~ on TV this morning.**

a. Are some cartons of ice cream in the freezer.

b. I don't use the subway because am afraid.

c. The prime minister she is the most popular leader in my country.

d. We tried to get in touch with the same manager whom we spoke to him earlier.

e. Recently have been a number of earthquakes in Turkey.

1. We visited an island where several ancient ruins are being excavated there.

2. In this city is difficult to find a high-paying job.

3. Beginning knitters they are often surprised that their fingers are sore at first.

4. Is a banyan tree in our backyard.

5. The CD that teaches Italian for opera lovers it was stolen from my backpack.

EXERCISE M3-2 ◆ Sentence structure

Before working this exercise, read sections M3-e and M3-f in *A Canadian Writer's Reference*, Fifth Edition.

Edit the following sentences for proper sentence structure. If a sentence is correct, write "correct" after it. Answers to lettered sentences appear in the back of the booklet. Example:

$$\text{She peeled } \cancel{\text{slowly}} \text{ the banana}\underset{\wedge}{/}^{\textit{slowly.}}$$

a. Although freshwater freezes at 0 °C, however ocean water freezes at −2 °C.

b. Because we switched cable packages, so our channel lineup has changed.

c. The competitor mounted confidently his skateboard.

d. My sister performs well the *legong*, a Balinese dance.

e. Because product development is behind schedule, we will have to launch the product next spring.

1. The teller counted methodically the pile of one-dollar coins.

2. I gasped when I saw lightning strike repeatedly the barn.

3. Although hockey is traditionally a winter sport, but many towns offer skills programs all year long.

4. Because the plane is amphibious, so it can land on the lake or on the airstrip nearby.

5. A surveyor determined quickly the boundaries of the property.

Hacker/Sommers, *Exercises for A Canadian Writer's Reference*, 5th ed. (Boston: Bedford, 2012)

EXERCISE M4-1 ◆ Present versus past participles

Before working this exercise, read section M4-a in *A Canadian Writer's Reference*, Fifth Edition.

Edit the following sentences for proper use of present and past participles. If a sentence is correct, write "correct" after it. Answers to lettered sentences appear in the back of the booklet. Example:

> *excited*
> **Danielle and Monica were very ~~exciting~~ to be going to a Broadway show for the first time.**
>   ^

a.   Listening to everyone's complaints all day was irritated.

b.   The long flight to Singapore was exhausted.

c.   His skill at chess is amazing.

d.   After a great deal of research, the scientist made a fascinated discovery.

e.   That blackout was one of the most frightened experiences I've ever had.

1.   I couldn't concentrate on my homework because I was distracted.

2.   The directions to the new board game seem extremely complicating.

3.   How interested are you in visiting Old Fort York?

4.   The aerial view of the devastated villages was depressing.

5.   The lecturer spoke slowly, but the students were still confusing.

Hacker/Sommers, *Exercises for A Canadian Writer's Reference*, 5th ed. (Boston: Bedford, 2012)

M4-1 | Present versus past participles   **59**

EXERCISE M4-2 ◆ Order of cumulative adjectives

Before working this exercise, read section M4-b in *A Canadian Writer's Reference*, Fifth Edition.

Referring to the chart on page 252 in the handbook, arrange the following modifiers and nouns in their proper order. Answers to lettered items appear in the back of the booklet. Example:

> *two new French racing bicycles*
> **new, French, two, bicycles, racing**

    a.   sculpture, new, an, Vietnamese, attractive

    b.   dedicated, a, priest, Catholic

    c.   old, her, sweater, blue, wool

    d.   delicious, Joe's, Scandinavian, bread

    e.   many, boxes, jewellery, antique, beautiful

    1.   oval, nine, brass, lamps, miniature

    2.   several, yellow, tulips, tiny

    3.   the, tree, gingko, yellow, ancient, Mongolian

    4.   courtyard, a, square, small, brick

    5.   charming, restaurants, Latvian, several

Hacker/Sommers, *Exercises for A Canadian Writer's Reference*, 5th ed. (Boston: Bedford, 2012)

EXERCISE M5-1 ◆ Prepositions showing time and place

Before working this exercise, read section M5-a in *A Canadian Writer's Reference*, Fifth Edition.

In the following sentences, replace prepositions that are not used correctly. You may need to refer to the chart on page 253 in the handbook. If a sentence is correct, write "correct" after it. Answers to lettered sentences appear in the back of the booklet. Example:

>   *at*
> **The play begins ~~on~~ 7:20 p.m.**
>   ^

a.   Whenever we eat at the Centreville Café, we sit at a small table on the corner of the room.

b.   In the 1990s, entrepreneurs created new online businesses in record numbers.

c.   In Thursday, Nancy will attend her first home repair class at the community centre.

d.   Alex began looking for her lost mitten in another location.

e.   We decided to go to a restaurant because there was no fresh food on the refrigerator.

1.   I like walking at my neighbourhood in night because I can always see stars.

2.   If the train is on time, it will arrive downtown on eleven o'clock at the morning.

3.   In the corner of the room there is a large bookcase with a pair of small Russian dolls standing at the top shelf.

4.   She licked the stamp, stuck it in the envelope, put the envelope on her pocket, and walked to the nearest mailbox.

5.   The mailbox was in the intersection of Laidlaw Avenue and Williams Street.

Hacker/Sommers, *Exercises for A Canadian Writer's Reference*, 5th ed. (Boston: Bedford, 2012)

M5-1 | Prepositions showing time and place   **61**

EXERCISE P1-1 ◆ The comma: independent clauses, introductory elements

Before working this exercise, read sections P1-a and P1-b in *A Canadian Writer's Reference*, Fifth Edition.

Add or delete commas where necessary in the following sentences. If a sentence is correct, write "correct" after it. Answers to lettered sentences appear in the back of the booklet. Example:

> **Because we had been saving moulding for a few weeks, we had enough wood**
> **   ^**
> **to frame all thirty paintings.**

a. Alisa brought the injured bird home, and fashioned a splint out of Popsicle sticks for its wing.

b. Considered a classic of early animation *The Adventures of Prince Achmed* used hand-cut silhouettes against coloured backgrounds.

c. If you complete the evaluation form and return it within two weeks you will receive a free breakfast during your next stay.

d. After retiring from ballet in 1997, award-winning dancer Karen Kain went on to become the artistic director of the National Ballet of Canada.

e. Roger had always wanted a handmade violin but he couldn't afford one.

1. While I was driving a huge delivery truck ran through a red light.

2. He pushed the car beyond the tollgate, and poured a bucket of water on the smoking hood.

3. Lit by bright halogen lamps hundreds of origami birds sparkled like diamonds in sunlight.

4. As the first chord sounded, Aileen knew that her spirits were about to rise.

5. Many musicians of Bach's time played several instruments but few mastered them as early or played with as much expression as Bach.

Hacker/Sommers, *Exercises for A Canadian Writer's Reference*, 5th ed. (Boston: Bedford, 2012)

EXERCISE P1-2 ◆ The comma: independent clauses, introductory elements

Before working this exercise, read sections P1-a and P1-b in *A Canadian Writer's Reference*, Fifth Edition.

Add or delete commas where necessary in the following sentences. If a sentence is correct, write "correct" after it. Answers to lettered sentences appear in the back of the booklet. Example:

> **The car had been sitting idle for a month, so the battery was completely dead.**
> ^

a. J. R. R. Tolkien finished writing his draft of *The Lord of the Rings* trilogy in 1949 but the first book in the series wasn't published until 1954.

b. In the first two minutes of its ascent the space shuttle had broken the sound barrier and reached a height of over forty kilometres.

c. German shepherds can be gentle guide dogs or they can be fierce attack dogs.

d. Some former professional cyclists claim that the use of performance-enhancing drugs is widespread in cycling and they argue that no rider can be competitive without doping.

e. As an intern, I learned most aspects of the broadcasting industry but I never learned about fundraising.

1. To be considered for the position candidates must demonstrate initiative and strong communication skills.

2. The cinematic lighting effect known as *chiaroscuro* was first used in German Expressionist filmmaking, and was later seen in American film noir.

3. Reptiles are cold-blooded and they are covered with scales.

4. Using a variety of techniques, advertisers grab the audience's attention and imprint their messages onto consumers' minds.

5. By the end of the first quarter the operating budget will be available online.

EXERCISE P1-3 ◆ The comma: series, coordinate adjectives

Before working this exercise, read sections P1-c and P1-d in *A Canadian Writer's Reference*, Fifth Edition.

Add or delete commas where necessary in the following sentences. If a sentence is correct, write "correct" after it. Answers to lettered sentences appear in the back of the booklet. Example:

> We gathered our essentials, took off for the great outdoors, and ignored the fact that
>
> it was Friday the 13th.

a. The cold impersonal atmosphere of the university was unbearable.

b. An ambulance threaded its way through police cars, fire trucks and curious onlookers.

c. The *1812 Overture* is a stirring, magnificent piece of music.

d. After two broken arms, three cracked ribs and one concussion, Ken quit the varsity football team.

e. My cat's pupils had constricted to small black shining slits.

1. We prefer our staff to be orderly, prompt and efficient.

2. For breakfast the children ordered cornflakes, English muffins with peanut butter and cherry Cokes.

3. It was a small, unimportant part, but I was happy to have it.

4. Cyril was clad in a luminous orange rain suit and a brilliant white helmet.

5. Animation master Hironobu Sakaguchi makes computer-generated scenes look realistic, vivid and seductive.

Hacker/Sommers, *Exercises for A Canadian Writer's Reference*, 5th ed. (Boston: Bedford, 2012)

EXERCISE P1-4 ◆ The comma: series, coordinate adjectives

Before working this exercise, read sections P1-c and P1-d in *A Canadian Writer's Reference*, Fifth Edition.

Add or delete commas where necessary in the following sentences. If a sentence is correct, write "correct" after it. Answers to lettered sentences appear in the back of the booklet. Example:

> **Good social workers excel in patience, diplomacy, and positive thinking.**
> ^

a. NASA's rovers on Mars are equipped with special cameras that can take close-up high-resolution pictures of the terrain.

b. A baseball player achieves the triple crown by having the highest batting average, the most home runs, and the most runs batted in during the regular season.

c. If it does not get enough sunlight, a healthy green lawn can turn into a shriveled brown mess within a matter of days.

d. Love, vengeance, greed and betrayal are common themes in Western literature.

e. Many experts believe that shark attacks on surfers are a result of the sharks' mistaking surfboards for small, injured seals.

1. During his service in World War I, John McCrae was gassed near Ypres, wrote "In Flanders Fields" and fell ill and died of pneumonia.

2. Milk that comes from grass-fed steroid-free cows has been gaining market share.

3. The film makes three main points about global warming: It is real, it is the result of human activity, and it should not be ignored.

4. The three, handmade, turquoise bracelets brought in the most money at the charity auction.

5. Matisse is well known for vibrant colourful prints that have been reproduced extensively on greeting cards and posters.

Hacker/Sommers, *Exercises for A Canadian Writer's Reference*, 5th ed. (Boston: Bedford, 2012)

P1-4 | The comma: series, coordinate adjectives 65

EXERCISE P1-5 ◆ The comma: nonrestrictive elements

Before working this exercise, read section P1-e in *A Canadian Writer's Reference*, Fifth Edition.

Add or delete commas where necessary in the following sentences. If a sentence is correct, write "correct" after it. Answers to lettered sentences appear in the back of the booklet. Example:

> **My youngest sister, who plays left wing on the soccer team, now lives at Otter Point,**
> **a beach house near Sooke.**

a. Choreographer Louise Bédard's best-known work *Enfin vous zestes*, is more than just a crowd pleaser.

b. Marie Chouinard's contemporary ballet *24 Preludes by Chopin* is being performed by the National Ballet of Canada. [*Chouinard has choreographed more than one contemporary ballet.*]

c. The glass sculptor sifting through hot red sand explained her technique to the other glassmakers. [*There is more than one glass sculptor.*]

d. A member of an organization, that provides job training for teens, was also appointed to the education commission.

e. Brian Eno who began his career as a rock musician turned to meditative compositions in the late 1970s.

1. I had the pleasure of talking to a woman who had just returned from India where she had lived for ten years.

2. Patrick's oldest sister Fiona graduated from MIT with a degree in aerospace engineering.

3. The artist painting a portrait of Aung San Suu Kyi, the Burmese civil rights leader, was once a political prisoner himself.

4. *When You Were Small*, the 2007 Marilyn Baillie Picture Book Award winner, is my nephew's favourite book.

5. The flame crawled up a few blades of grass to reach a low-hanging palmetto branch which quickly ignited.

Hacker/Sommers, *Exercises for A Canadian Writer's Reference*, 5th ed. (Boston: Bedford, 2012)

EXERCISE P1-6 ◆ Major uses of the comma

Before working this exercise, read sections P1-a to P1-e in *A Canadian Writer's Reference*, Fifth Edition.

Add or delete commas where necessary. If a sentence is correct, write "correct" after it. Answers to lettered sentences appear in the back of the booklet. Example:

> **Even though Pavel had studied Nigella Lawson's recipes for a week, he underestimated how long it would take to juice two hundred lemons.**

a. Cricket which originated in England is also popular in Australia, South Africa and India.

b. At the sound of the starting pistol the horses surged forward toward the first obstacle, a sharp incline one metre high.

c. After seeing an exhibition of Western art Gerhard Richter escaped from East Berlin, and smuggled out many of his notebooks.

d. Corrie's new wet suit has an intricate, blue pattern.

e. The cookies will keep for two weeks in sturdy airtight containers.

1. Research on Andean condors has shown that high levels of the pesticide chlorinated hydrocarbon can cause the thinning of eggshells.

2. Founded in 1899 Frontier College brought education to Canadian labour camps.

3. Aunt Emilia was an impossible demanding guest.

4. The French Mirage, a high-tech fighter, is an astonishing machine to fly.

5. At the bottom of the ship's rusty hold sat several, well-preserved trunks, reminders of a bygone era of sea travel.

Hacker/Sommers, *Exercises for A Canadian Writer's Reference*, 5th ed. (Boston: Bedford, 2012)

P1-6 | Major uses of the comma   **67**

EXERCISE P1-7 ◆ All uses of the comma

Before working this exercise, read section P1 in *A Canadian Writer's Reference*, Fifth Edition.

Add or delete commas where necessary in the following sentences. If a sentence is correct, write "correct" after it. Answers to lettered sentences appear in the back of the booklet. Example:

> **"Yes, dear, you can have dessert," my mother said.**
>   ^

a. On January 15, 2008 our office moved to 29 Commonwealth Avenue, Toronto ON M1K 4J8.

b. The coach having bawled us out thoroughly, we left the locker room with his harsh words ringing in our ears.

c. Ms. Carlson you are a valued customer whose satisfaction is very important to us.

d. Mr. Mundy was born on July 22, 1939 in Alberta, where his family had lived for four generations.

e. Her board poised at the edge of the half-pipe, Nina waited her turn to drop in.

1. Prime Minister Trudeau's intention was to unite Canada, not to strengthen separatism.

2. For centuries people believed that Greek culture had developed in isolation from the world. Today however scholars are acknowledging the contributions made by Egypt and the Middle East.

3. Putting together a successful fundraiser, Patricia discovered, requires creativity and good timing.

4. Fortunately science is creating many alternatives to research performed on animals.

5. While the machine was printing the oversize paper jammed.

Hacker/Sommers, *Exercises for A Canadian Writer's Reference*, 5th ed. (Boston: Bedford, 2012)

EXERCISE P2-1 ◆ Unnecessary commas

Before working this exercise, read section P2 in *A Canadian Writer's Reference*, Fifth Edition.

Delete any unnecessary commas in the following sentences. If a sentence is correct, write "correct" after it. Answers to lettered sentences appear in the back of the booklet. Example:

> **In his Silk Road Project, Yo-Yo Ma incorporates work by musicians such as/ Kayhan Kahlor and Richard Danielpour.**

a. After the morning rains cease, the swimmers emerge from their cottages.

b. Tricia's first artwork was a bright, blue, clay dolphin.

c. Some modern musicians, (the group Beyond the Pale is an example) blend several cultural traditions into a unique sound.

d. Myra liked hot, spicy foods such as, chili, kung pao chicken, and buffalo wings.

e. On the display screen, was a soothing pattern of light and shadow.

1. Mesquite, the hardest of the softwoods, grows primarily in the US Southwest.

2. Jolie's parents encouraged independent thinking, but required respect for others' opinions.

3. The border guards told their sergeant, that their heat-sensing equipment was malfunctioning.

4. The streets that three hours later would be bumper to bumper with commuters, were quiet and empty except for a few prowling cats.

5. Some first-year architecture students, expect to design intricate structures immediately.

Hacker/Sommers, *Exercises for A Canadian Writer's Reference*, 5th ed. (Boston: Bedford, 2012)

P2-1 | Unnecessary commas **69**

EXERCISE P2-2 ◆ Unnecessary commas

Before working this exercise, read section P2 in *A Canadian Writer's Reference*, Fifth Edition.

Delete unnecessary commas in the following passage.

Each summer since 1980, Montreal has hosted the Montreal International Jazz Festival, an event that celebrates jazz music and musicians. Although, its name includes only jazz, it typically features a wide variety of musical styles such as, electronica, Latin, big band, classical, and, rock and roll. Famous musicians who have appeared regularly at the Jazz Festival, include Oscar Peterson, B. B. King, and Aretha Franklin. Every year, the festival hosts more than 650 concerts, which are seen by close to 2.5 million visitors. Ten outdoor stages are located throughout the festival, and offer 450 free concerts. In 2009, the festival marked its thirtieth anniversary. Fans, who could not attend the festival, still enjoyed the music by buying CDs, and watching videos of the performances online.

Hacker/Sommers, *Exercises for A Canadian Writer's Reference*, 5th ed. (Boston: Bedford, 2012)

EXERCISE P3-1 ◆ The semicolon and the comma

Before working this exercise, read sections P3-a to P3-c and review sections P1 and P2 in *A Canadian Writer's Reference*, Fifth Edition.

Add commas or semicolons where needed in the following well-known quotations. If a sentence is correct, write "correct" after it. Answers to lettered sentences appear in the back of the booklet. Example:

> **If an animal does something, we call it instinct; if we do the same thing, we call it intelligence.** —**Will Cuppy**

a. Do not ask me to be kind just ask me to act as though I were.   —Jules Renard

b. If I ever have a conflict between art and nature I let art win.   —Robert Bateman

c. When I get a little money I buy books if any is left I buy food and clothes.

—Desiderius Erasmus

d. The basis of my approach as a teacher has always been that we participate in society by means of our imagination or the quality of our social vision.   —Northrop Frye

e. I detest life-insurance agents they always argue that I shall some day die.

—Stephen Leacock

1. Standing in the middle of the road is very dangerous you get knocked down by the traffic from both sides.   —Margaret Thatcher

2. He knew his limitations, which is more than I can say for the rest of us.

—Pierre Elliott Trudeau

3. Once the children were in the house the air became more vivid and more heated every object in the house grew more alive.   —Mary Gordon

4. If death is a debt we must all pay he paid it before he owed it.   —Adrienne Clarkson

5. I've been rich and I've been poor rich is better.   —Sophie Tucker

Name _____ Section _____ Date _____

EXERCISE P3-2 ◆ The semicolon and the comma

Before working this exercise, read sections P3-a to P3-c and review sections P1 and P2 in *A Canadian Writer's Reference*, Fifth Edition.

Edit the following sentences to correct errors in the use of the comma and the semicolon. If a sentence is correct, write "correct" after it. Answers to lettered sentences appear in the back of the booklet. Example:

> **Love is blind; envy has its eyes wide open.**
>   ^

a. Strong black coffee will not sober you up, the truth is that time is the only way to get alcohol out of your system.

b. Margaret was not surprised to see hail and vivid lightning, conditions had been right for violent weather all day.

c. There is often a fine line between right and wrong; good and bad; truth and deception.

d. My mother always says that you can't learn common sense; either you're born with it or you're not.

e. Severe, unremitting pain is a ravaging force; especially when the patient tries to hide it from others.

1. Another delicious dish is the chef's special; a roasted duck rubbed with spices and stuffed with wild rice.

2. Martin Luther King Jr. had not always intended to be a preacher, initially, he had planned to become a lawyer.

3. We all assumed that the thief had been Jean's boyfriend; even though we had seen him only from the back.

4. The Victorians avoided the subject of sex but were obsessed with death, a hundred years later, people were obsessed with sex but avoided thinking about death.

5. Some educators believe that Black history should be taught in separate courses, others prefer to see it integrated into survey courses.

Hacker/Sommers, *Exercises for A Canadian Writer's Reference*, 5th ed. (Boston: Bedford, 2012)

EXERCISE P3-3 ◆ The colon, the semicolon, and the comma

Before working this exercise, read sections P3-d to P3-f and review sections P1 and P3-a to P3-c in *A Canadian Writer's Reference*, Fifth Edition.

Edit the following sentences to correct errors in the use of the comma, the semicolon, or the colon. If a sentence is correct, write "correct" after it. Answers to lettered sentences appear in the back of the booklet. Example:

> **Lifting the cover gently, Luca found the source of the odd sound/: a marble in the gears.**
> ^

a. We always looked forward to Thanksgiving in Winnipeg: It was our only chance to see our Grady cousins.

b. If we have come to fight, we are far too few, if we have come to die, we are far too many.

c. The travel package includes: a round-trip ticket to Athens, a cruise through the Cyclades, and all hotel accommodations.

d. The news article portrays the land use proposal as reckless; although 62 percent of the town's residents support it.

e. Psychologists Kindlon and Thompson (2000) offer parents a simple starting point for raising male children, "Teach boys that there are many ways to be a man" (p. 256).

1. Harry Potter prevails against pain and evil for one reason, his heart is pure.

2. While travelling through France, Rose visited: the Loire Valley, Chartres, the Louvre, and the McDonald's stand at the foot of the Eiffel Tower.

3. There are three types of leave; annual leave, used for vacations, sick leave, used for medical appointments and illness, and personal leave, used for a variety of personal reasons.

4. American poet Carl Sandburg once asked these three questions, "Who paid for my freedom? What was the price? And am I somehow beholden?"

5. Amelie had four goals: to be encouraging, to be effective, to be efficient, and to be elegant.

Hacker/Sommers, *Exercises for A Canadian Writer's Reference*, 5th ed. (Boston: Bedford, 2012)

P3-3 | The colon, the semicolon, and the comma **73**

EXERCISE P4-1 ◆ The apostrophe

Before working this exercise, read section P4 in *A Canadian Writer's Reference*, Fifth Edition.

Edit the following sentences to correct errors in the use of the apostrophe. If a sentence is correct, write "correct" after it. Answers to lettered sentences appear in the back of the booklet. Example:

> *Richard's*
> **Our favourite barbecue restaurant is Poor ~~Richards~~ Ribs.**
> ^

a. This diet will improve almost anyone's health.

b. The innovative shoe fastener was inspired by the designers young grandson.

c. Each days menu features a different European country's dish.

d. Sue worked overtime to increase her families earnings.

e. Ms. Jacobs is unwilling to listen to students complaints about computer failures.

1. Siddhartha sat by the river and listened to its many voices.

2. Three teenage son's can devour about as much food as four full-grown field hands. The only difference is that they dont do half as much work.

3. The small biotech company has contracts with NASA and other government agency's.

4. Patience and humour are key tools in a travellers survival kit.

5. My sister-in-law's colourful patchwork quilts are being shown at the Confederation Centre Art Gallery and Museum.

Hacker/Sommers, *Exercises for A Canadian Writer's Reference*, 5th ed. (Boston: Bedford, 2012)

EXERCISE P4-2 ◆ The apostrophe

Before working this exercise, read section P4 in *A Canadian Writer's Reference*, Fifth Edition.

Edit the following passage to correct errors in the use of the apostrophe.

Its never too soon to start holiday shopping. In fact, some people choose to start shopping as early as January, when last seasons leftover's are priced at their lowest. Many stores try to lure customers in with promise's of savings up to 90 percent. Their main objective, of course, is to make way for next years inventory. The big problem with postholiday shopping, though, is that there isn't much left to choose from. Store's shelves have been picked over by last-minute shoppers desperately searching for gifts. The other problem is that its hard to know what to buy so far in advance. Next year's hot items are anyones guess. But proper timing, mixed with lot's of luck and determination, can lead to good purchases at great price's.

EXERCISE P5-1 ◆ Quotation marks

Before working this exercise, read section P5 in *A Canadian Writer's Reference*, Fifth Edition.

Add or delete quotation marks as needed and make any other necessary changes in punctuation in the following sentences. If a sentence is correct, write "correct" after it. Answers to lettered sentences appear in the back of the booklet. Example:

> **Gandhi once said, "An eye for an eye only ends up making the whole world blind."**
>   ^   ^

a. As for the advertisement "Sailors have more fun", if you consider chipping paint and swabbing decks fun, then you will have plenty of it.

b. Even after forty minutes of discussion, our class could not agree on an interpretation of Robert Frost's poem "The Road Not Taken."

c. After winning the lottery, Juanita said that "she would give half the money to charity."

d. After the movie, Vicki said, "The reviewer called this flick "trash of the first order." I guess you can't believe everything you read."

e. "Cleaning your house while your kids are still growing," said Phyllis Diller, "is like shoveling the walk before it stops snowing."

1. "That's the most beautiful seashell I've ever seen!", shouted Alexa.

2. "Get your head in the game, and the rest will come" advised the coach just before the whistle.

3. Gloria Steinem once twisted an old proverb like this, "A woman without a man is like a fish without a bicycle."

4. "Even when freshly washed and relieved of all obvious confections," said Fran Lebowitz, "children tend to be sticky."

5. Have you heard the Cowboy Junkies' rendition of Hank Williams's "I'm So Lonesome I Could Cry?"

Hacker/Sommers, *Exercises for A Canadian Writer's Reference*, 5th ed. (Boston: Bedford, 2012)

EXERCISE P5-2 ◆ Quotation marks

Before working this exercise, read section P5 in *A Canadian Writer's Reference*, Fifth Edition.

Add or delete quotation marks as needed and make any other necessary changes in punctuation in the following passage. Citations should conform to MLA style (see MLA-4a).

In his article The Moment of Truth, former vice president Al Gore argues that global warming is a genuine threat to life on Earth and that we must act now to avoid catastrophe. Gore calls our situation a "true *planetary emergency*" and cites scientific evidence of the greenhouse effect and its consequences (170-71). "What is at stake, Gore insists, is the survival of our civilization and the habitability of the Earth (197)." With such a grim predicament at hand, Gore questions why so many political and economic leaders are reluctant to act. "Is it simply more convenient to ignore the warnings," he asks (171)?

The crisis, of course, will not go away if we just pretend it isn't there. Gore points out that in Chinese two symbols form the character for the word crisis. The first of those symbols means "danger", and the second means "opportunity." The danger we face, he claims, is accompanied by "unprecedented opportunity." (172) Gore contends that throughout history we have won battles against seemingly unbeatable evils such as slavery and fascism and that we did so by facing the truth and choosing the moral high ground. Gore's final appeal is to our humanity:

> "Ultimately, [the fight to end global warming] is not about any scientific discussion or political dialogue; it is about who we are as human beings. It is about our capacity to transcend our limitations, to rise to this new occasion. To see with our hearts, as well as our heads, the response that is now called for." (244)

Gore feels that the fate of our world rests in our own hands, and his hope is that we will make the choice to save the planet.

Source of quotations: Al Gore; "The Moment of Truth"; *Vanity Fair* May 2006: 170+; print.

EXERCISE P6-1 ◆ The period, the question mark, and the exclamation point

Before working this exercise, read section P6-a in *A Canadian Writer's Reference*, Fifth Edition.

Add appropriate end punctuation in the following paragraph.

Although I am generally rational, I am superstitious I never walk under ladders or put shoes on the table If I spill the salt, I go into frenzied calisthenics picking up the grains and tossing them over my left shoulder As a result of these curious activities, I've always wondered whether knowing the roots of superstitions would quell my irrational responses Superstition has it, for example, that one should never place a hat on the bed This superstition arises from a time when head lice were common and placing a guest's hat on the bed stood a good chance of spreading lice through the host's bed Doesn't this make good sense And doesn't it stand to reason that, if I know that my guests don't have lice, I shouldn't care where their hats go Of course it does It is fair to ask, then, whether I have changed my ways and place hats on beds Are you kidding I wouldn't put a hat on a bed if my life depended on it

Hacker/Sommers, *Exercises for A Canadian Writer's Reference*, 5th ed. (Boston: Bedford, 2012)

EXERCISE P6-2 ◆ Other punctuation marks

Before working this exercise, read sections P6-b to P6-d in *A Canadian Writer's Reference*, Fifth Edition.

Edit the following sentences to correct errors in punctuation, focusing especially on appropriate use of the dash, parentheses, brackets, ellipsis mark, and slash. If a sentence is correct, write "correct" after it. Answers to lettered sentences appear in the back of the booklet. Example:

> **Social insects/ —bees, for example/ —are able to communicate complicated**
> **^   ^**
> **messages to one another.**

a.   A client has left his/her cell phone in our conference room.

b.   The films we made of Kilauea—on our trip to Hawaii Volcanoes National Park—illustrate a typical spatter cone eruption.

c.   Greg selected the pass/fail option for Chemistry 101.

d.   Masahiro poked through his backpack—laptop, digital camera, guidebook—to make sure he was ready for a day's study at the Ryoanji Temple garden.

e.   Of three engineering fields, chemical, mechanical, and materials, Keegan chose materials engineering for its application to toy manufacturing.

1.   The old Valentine verse we used to chant says it all: "Sugar is sweet, / And so are you."

2.   In studies in which mothers gazed down at their infants in their cribs but remained facially unresponsive, for example, not smiling, laughing, or showing any change of expression, the infants responded with intense weariness and eventual withdrawal.

3.   There are three points of etiquette in poker: 1. always allow someone else to cut the cards, 2. don't forget to ante up, and 3. never stack your chips.

4.   In *Lifeboat*, Alfred Hitchcock appears [some say without his knowledge] in a newspaper advertisement for weight loss.

5.   The writer Chitra Divakaruni explained her work with other Indian American immigrants: "Many women who came to Maitri [a women's support group in San Francisco] needed to know simple things like opening a bank account or getting citizenship. . . . Many women in Maitri spoke English, but their English was functional rather than emotional. They needed someone who understands their problems and speaks their language."

Hacker/Sommers, *Exercises for A Canadian Writer's Reference*, 5th ed. (Boston: Bedford, 2012)

P6-2 | Other punctuation marks   **79**

EXERCISE P7-1 ◆ Spelling

Before working this exercise, read sections P7-a and P7-b in *A Canadian Writer's Reference*, Fifth Edition.

The following memo has been run through a spell checker. Proofread it carefully, editing the spelling and typographical errors that remain.

November 3, 2010

To: Patricia Wise

From: Constance Mayhew

Subject: Express Tours annual report

Thank you for agreeing to draft the annual report for Express Tours. Before you begin you're work, let me outline the initial steps.

First, its essential for you to include brief profiles of top management. Early next week, I'll provide profiles for all manages accept Samuel Heath, who's biographical information is being revised. You should edit these profiles carefully and than format them according to the enclosed instructions. We may ask you to include other employee's profiles at some point.

Second, you should arrange to get complete financial information for fiscal year 2010 from our comptroller, Richard Chang. (Helen Boyes, to, can provide the necessary figures.) When you get this information, precede according tot he plans we discuss in yesterday's meeting. By the way, you will notice from the figures that the sale of our Charterhouse division did not significantly effect net profits.

Third, you should submit first draft of the report by December 15. I assume that you won a laser printer, but if you don't, you can e-mail a file and we'll print out a draft here. Of coarse, you should proofread you writing.

I am quiet pleased that you can take on this project. If I can answers questions, don't hesitate to call.

Hacker/Sommers, *Exercises for A Canadian Writer's Reference*, 5th ed. (Boston: Bedford, 2012)

EXERCISE P7-2 ◆ The hyphen

Before working this exercise, read sections P7-c to P7-h in *A Canadian Writer's Reference*, Fifth Edition.

Edit the following sentences to correct errors in hyphenation. If a sentence is correct, write "correct" after it. Answers to lettered sentences appear in the back of the booklet. Example:

> **Zola's first readers were scandalized by his slice‿of‿life novels.**
>   ^   ^

a.   Gold is the seventy-ninth element in the periodic table.

b.   The swiftly-moving tugboat pulled alongside the barge and directed it away from the oil spill in the harbour.

c.   The Moche were a pre-Columbian people who established a sophisticated culture in ancient Peru.

d.   Your dog is well-known in our neighbourhood.

e.   Road-blocks were set up along all the major highways leading out of the city.

1.   We knew we were driving too fast when our tires skidded on the rain slick surface.

2.   The Black Death reduced the population of some medieval villages by two thirds.

3.   Sewing forty-eight sequined tutus for the ballet recital nearly made Karyn cross-eyed.

4.   Olivia had hoped to find a pay as you go plan to finance the construction of her observatory.

5.   Gail Sheehy writes that at age twenty five many people assume that the choices they make are irrevocable.

Hacker/Sommers, *Exercises for A Canadian Writer's Reference*, 5th ed. (Boston: Bedford, 2012)

P7-2 | The hyphen   **81**

EXERCISE P8-1 ◆ Capital letters

Before working this exercise, read section P8 in *A Canadian Writer's Reference*, Fifth Edition.

Edit the following sentences to correct errors in capitalization. If a sentence is correct, write "correct" after it. Answers to lettered sentences appear in the back of the booklet. Example:

$$\begin{array}{cccccc} L & G & B & K & H & P \end{array}$$

On our trip to the West we visited ~~l~~ions ~~g~~ate ~~b~~ridge and ~~k~~icking ~~h~~orse ~~p~~ass.

a. Assistant dean Shirin Ahmadi recommended offering more world language courses.

b. We went to the Tarragon Theatre to see a production of *How It Works.*

c. Kalindi has an ambitious semester, studying differential calculus, classical hebrew, brochure design, and greek literature.

d. Lydia's Aunt and Uncle make modular houses as beautiful as modernist works of art.

e. We amused ourselves on the long flight by discussing how Spring in Kyoto stacks up against Summer in London.

1. When the truck will not start, I try a few tricks with the ignition key: Jiggling it to the left, pulling it out five millimetres, and gently pulling down on it.

2. When you slowly bake a clove of garlic, the most amazing thing happens: It loses its bitter tang and becomes sweet and buttery.

3. After World War II, aunt Helena left Poland to study in Italy.

4. When we drove through the American south last year, we enjoyed stopping at the peanut stands along the road.

5. Following in his sister's footsteps, Leonid is pursuing a degree in Marketing Research.

Hacker/Sommers, *Exercises for A Canadian Writer's Reference,* 5th ed. (Boston: Bedford, 2012)

EXERCISE P9-1 ◆ Abbreviations

Before working this exercise, read sections P9-a to P9-e in *A Canadian Writer's Reference*, Fifth Edition.

Edit the following sentences to correct errors in abbreviations. If a sentence is correct, write "correct" after it. Answers to lettered sentences appear in the back of the booklet. Example:

Christmas   *Tuesday.*

This year ~~Xmas~~ will fall on a ~~Tues.~~

a. Since its inception, the CBC has maintained a consistently high standard of radio and
    television broadcasting.

b. Some combat soldiers are trained by govt. diplomats to be sensitive to issues of culture,
    history, and religion.

c. Mahatma Gandhi inspired many modern leaders, including Martin Luther King Jr.

d. How many kg have you lost since you began lifting weights and adding protein to your diet?

e. Denzil spent all night studying for his psych. exam.

1. My favourite prof., Dr. Barker, is on sabbatical this semester.

2. When we visited UBC in early September, we were charmed by the lull of summer crickets
    in Pacific Spirit Park.

3. Some historians think that the New Testament was completed by AD 100.

4. My mother's birthday was on Fri. the 13th this year.

5. Some first-time users of Flash panic before the complex menus—i.e., they develop a blank
    stare and the tingling of a migraine.

Hacker/Sommers, *Exercises for A Canadian Writer's
Reference*, 5th ed. (Boston: Bedford, 2012)

P9-1 | Abbreviations **83**

EXERCISE P9-2 ◆ Numbers

Before working this exercise, read sections P9-f and P9-g in *A Canadian Writer's Reference*, Fifth Edition.

Edit the following sentences to correct errors in the use of numbers. If a sentence is correct, write "correct" after it. Answers to lettered sentences appear in the back of the booklet. Example:

$3.06
By the end of the evening, Ashanti had only ~~three dollars and six cents~~ left.
                                              ^

a. The carpenters located 3 maple timbers, 21 sheets of cherry, and 10 oblongs of polished ebony for the theatre set.

b. The program's cost is well over one billion dollars.

c. The score was tied at 5–5 when the momentum shifted and carried the Standards to a decisive 12–5 win.

d. 8 students in the class won awards at the district art fair.

e. The Canadian National Vimy Memorial in France had eleven thousand two hundred and eighty-five names inscribed on it when it was unveiled in 1936.

1. One of my favourite scenes in Shakespeare is the property division scene in act 1 of *King Lear*.

2. The botany lecture will begin at precisely 3:30 p.m.

3. 35 percent of all gamers in Canada are women.

4. In two thousand twelve, the world population may reach 7 billion.

5. On a normal day, I spend at least 4 to 5 hours surfing the Internet.

Hacker/Sommers, *Exercises for A Canadian Writer's Reference*, 5th ed. (Boston: Bedford, 2012)

EXERCISE P10-1 ◆ Italics

Before working this exercise, read section P10 in *A Canadian Writer's Reference*, Fifth Edition.

Edit the following sentences to correct errors in the use of italics. If a sentence is correct, write "correct" after it. Answers to lettered sentences appear in the back of the booklet. Example:

> **We had a lively discussion about Gini Alhadeff's memoir *The Sun at Midday*. *Correct***

a.   Howard Hughes commissioned the Spruce Goose, a beautifully built but thoroughly impractical wooden aircraft.

b.   The old man *screamed* his anger, *shouting* to all of us, "I will not leave my money to you worthless layabouts!"

c.   I learned the Latin term ad infinitum from an old nursery rhyme about fleas: "Great fleas have little fleas upon their back to bite 'em, / Little fleas have lesser fleas and so on ad infinitum."

d.   Cinema audiences once gasped at hearing the word *damn* in *Gone with the Wind*.

e.   Neve Campbell's lifelong interest in ballet inspired her involvement in the film "The Company," which portrays a season with the Joffrey Ballet.

1.   Yasmina spent a year painting white flowers in imitation of Georgia O'Keeffe's Calla Lilies.

2.   On the monastery walls are murals depicting scenes from the book of Kings and the book of Proverbs.

3.   My per diem allowance was $175.

4.   Cecily watched in amazement as the tattoo artist made angles and swooping loops into the Gothic letter G.

5.   The blend of poetic lyrics and progressive instruments on Seal's "Human Being" makes it one of my favourite CDs.

Hacker/Sommers, *Exercises for A Canadian Writer's Reference*, 5th ed. (Boston: Bedford, 2012)

P10-1 | Italics   **85**

EXERCISE B1-1 ◆ Parts of speech: nouns

Before working this exercise, read section B1-a in *A Canadian Writer's Reference*, Fifth Edition.

Underline the nouns (and noun/adjectives) in the following sentences. Answers to lettered sentences appear in the back of the booklet. Example:

> The best <u>part</u> of <u>dinner</u> was the <u>chef's</u> newest <u>dessert.</u>

a.   The stage was set for a confrontation of biblical proportions.

b.   The courage of the mountain climber was an inspiration to the rescuers.

c.   The need to arrive before the guest of honour motivated us to navigate the thick fog.

d.   The defence lawyer made a final appeal to the jury.

e.   A national museum dedicated to women artists opened in 1987.

1.   Truthfulness is a virtue lacking in some public officials.

2.   The Wright Brothers used a wind tunnel to test their airplane designs.

3.   The miners' work clothes were clogged with fine black dust.

4.   Virginia Woolf wrote that women need their own income and their own space.

5.   The child's language was a charming combination of her father's English and her mother's French.

Hacker/Sommers, *Exercises for A Canadian Writer's Reference*, 5th ed. (Boston: Bedford, 2012)

EXERCISE B1-2 ◆ Parts of speech: pronouns

Before working this exercise, read section B1-b in *A Canadian Writer's Reference*, Fifth Edition.

Underline the pronouns (and pronoun/adjectives) in the following sentences. Answers to lettered sentences appear in the back of the booklet. Example:

> **We were intrigued by the video that the fifth graders produced as their**
>
> **final technology project.**

    a.   The premier's loyalty was his most appealing trait.

    b.   In the fall, the geese that fly south for the winter pass through our town in huge numbers.

    c.   Carl Sandburg once said that even he himself did not understand some of his poetry.

    d.   I appealed my parking ticket, but you did not get one.

    e.   Angela did not mind gossip as long as no one gossiped about her.

    1.   The Tigers stood unhappily in front of their dugout while the victorious Jaguars tossed their hats in the air.

    2.   Nothing fascinated the toddler like something that was not his.

    3.   We understood that we were expected to submit our dissertations in triplicate.

    4.   The trick-or-treaters helped themselves to their neighbours' candy.

    5.   She found herself peering into the mouth of a creepy cave.

EXERCISE B1-3 ◆ Parts of speech: verbs

Before working this exercise, read section B1-c in *A Canadian Writer's Reference*, Fifth Edition.

Underline the verbs in the following sentences, including helping verbs and particles. If a verb is part of a contraction (such as *is* in *isn't* or *would* in *I'd*), underline only the letters that represent the verb. Answers to lettered sentences appear in the back of the booklet. Example:

> **The ground under the pine trees <u>wasn't</u> wet from the rain.**

a.   My grandmother always told me a soothing story before bed.

b.   There were fifty apples on the tree before the frost killed them.

c.   Morton brought down the box of letters from the attic.

d.   Stay on the main road and you'll arrive at the base camp before us.

e.   The fish struggled vigorously but was trapped in the net.

1.   Do not bring up that issue again.

2.   Galileo lived the last years of his life under house arrest because of his revolutionary

     theories about the universe.

3.   Cynthia asked for a raise, but she didn't expect one immediately.

4.   We should plant the roses early this year.

5.   The documentary was engrossing. It humanized World War II.

Hacker/Sommers, *Exercises for A Canadian Writer's*
Reference, 5th ed. (Boston: Bedford, 2012)

EXERCISE B1-4 ◆ Parts of speech: adjectives and adverbs

Before working this exercise, read sections B1-d and B1-e in *A Canadian Writer's Reference*, Fifth Edition.

Underline the adjectives and circle the adverbs in the following sentences. If a word is a noun or pronoun functioning as an adjective, underline it and mark it as a noun/adjective or pronoun/adjective. Also treat the articles *a*, *an*, and *the* as adjectives. Answers to lettered sentences appear in the back of the booklet. Example:

> Finding <u>an</u> <u>available</u> room during <u>the</u> convention was (not) easy.

a. Generalizations lead to weak, unfocused essays.

b. The Spanish language is wonderfully flexible.

c. The wildflowers smelled especially fragrant after the steady rain.

d. I'd rather be slightly hot than bitterly cold.

e. The cat slept soundly in its wicker basket.

1. Success can be elusive to those who object to working hard.

2. After three hours, the discussion had dwindled from a lively sprint to a tedious crawl.

3. She made a fairly earnest attempt at solving the most difficult calculus problems.

4. The black bear sniffed eagerly at the broken honeycomb.

5. The bacteria in the dish grew steadily over twenty-four hours.

Hacker/Sommers, *Exercises for A Canadian Writer's Reference*, 5th ed. (Boston: Bedford, 2012)

B1-4 | Parts of speech: adjectives and adverbs   **89**

EXERCISE B2-1 ◆ Parts of sentences: subjects

Before working this exercise, read section B2-a in *A Canadian Writer's Reference*, Fifth Edition.

In the following sentences, underline the complete subject and write *SS* above the simple subject(s). If the subject is an understood *you*, insert *you* in parentheses. Answers to lettered sentences appear in the back of the booklet. Example:

> ┌─*SS*─┐   ┌─*SS*─┐
> **Parents and their children** often look alike.

a.   The hills and mountains seemed endless, and the snow atop them glistened.

b.   In foil fencing, points are scored by hitting an electronic target.

c.   Do not stand in the aisles or sit on the stairs.

d.   There were hundreds of fireflies in the open field.

e.   The evidence against the defendant was staggering.

1.   The size of the new building caused an uproar in the town.

2.   Eat heartily. You need your strength.

3.   In the opinion of the court, siblings must be kept together.

4.   All of the books in the old library smelled like mothballs.

5.   There were no tour buses at the customs booth.

Hacker/Sommers, *Exercises for A Canadian Writer's Reference*, 5th ed. (Boston: Bedford, 2012)

EXERCISE B2-2 ◆ Parts of sentences: subject complements and direct objects

Before working this exercise, read section B2-b in *A Canadian Writer's Reference*, Fifth Edition.

Label the subject complements and direct objects in the following sentences, using the labels *SC* and *DO*. If a subject complement or direct object consists of more than one word, bracket and label all of it. Answers to lettered sentences appear in the back of the booklet. Example:

$$\overbrace{}^{DO}$$

The sharp right turn confused most drivers.

a. Textbooks are expensive.

b. Samurai warriors never fear death.

c. Successful coaches always praise their players' efforts.

d. St. Petersburg was the capital of the Russian Empire for two centuries.

e. The medicine tasted bitter.

1. Solar flares emit UV radiation.

2. The friends' quarrel was damaging their relationship.

3. Feng shui is the practice of achieving harmony between the physical and the spiritual in one's environment.

4. A well-made advertisement captures viewers' attention.

5. The island's climate was neither too hot nor too rainy.

Hacker/Sommers, *Exercises for A Canadian Writer's Reference*, 5th ed. (Boston: Bedford, 2012)

B2-2 | Parts of sentences: subject complements and direct objects **91**

EXERCISE B2-3 ◆ Parts of sentences: objects and complements

Before working this exercise, read section B2-b in *A Canadian Writer's Reference*, Fifth Edition.

Each of the following sentences has either an indirect object followed by a direct object or a direct object followed by an object complement. Label the objects and complements, using the labels *IO*, *DO*, and *OC*. If an object or a complement consists of more than one word, bracket and label all of it. Answers to lettered sentences appear in the back of the booklet. Example:

$$\overset{\overbrace{\qquad\qquad DO \qquad\qquad}}{}\ \overset{\overbrace{OC}}{}$$

Most people consider their own experience normal.

a.   Stress can make adults and children weary.

b.   Zita has made community service her priority this year.

c.   Consider the work finished.

d.   We showed the agent our tickets, and she gave us boarding passes.

e.   The dining hall offered students healthy meal choices.

1.   Send the registrar your scholarship form today.

2.   The independent research institute gives its scholars the freedom to work without

     government or military interference.

3.   Computer viruses make networks vulnerable.

4.   Give me a book's title, and I can tell you the author.

5.   The dire forecast made us extremely cautious about riding out the storm at home.

Hacker/Sommers, *Exercises for A Canadian Writer's Reference*, 5th ed. (Boston: Bedford, 2012)

EXERCISE B3-1 ◆ Subordinate word groups: prepositional phrases

Before working this exercise, read section B3-a in *A Canadian Writer's Reference*, Fifth Edition.

Underline the prepositional phrases in the following sentences. Tell whether each one is an adjective phrase or an adverb phrase and what it modifies in the sentence. Answers to lettered sentences appear in the back of the booklet. Example:

> Flecks <u>of mica</u> glittered <u>in the new granite floor</u>. *(Adjective phrase modifying "Flecks"; adverb phrase modifying "glittered")*

a. In northern Italy, some people speak German as their first language.

b. William completed the hike through the thick forest with ease.

c. To my boss's dismay, I was late for work again.

d. The travelling exhibit of Mayan artifacts gave viewers new insight into pre-Columbian culture.

e. In 2002, the euro became the official currency in twelve European countries.

1. The Silk Road was an old trade route between China and other parts of the world.

2. Dough with too much flour yields heavy baked goods.

3. On one side of the barricades were revolutionary students; on the other was a government militia.

4. You can tell with just one whiff whether the milk is fresh.

5. At first, we couldn't decide whether to take the car or the train, but in the end we decided to take the train.

Hacker/Sommers, *Exercises for A Canadian Writer's Reference*, 5th ed. (Boston: Bedford, 2012)

B3-1 | Subordinate word groups: prepositional phrases **93**

EXERCISE B3-2 ◆ Subordinate word groups: verbal phrases

Before working this exercise, read section B3-b in *A Canadian Writer's Reference*, Fifth Edition.

Underline the verbal phrases in the following sentences. Tell whether each phrase is participial, gerund, or infinitive and how each is used in the sentence. Answers to lettered sentences appear in the back of the booklet. Example:

> Do you want <u>to watch that documentary</u>? *(Infinitive phrase used as direct object of "Do want")*

a. Updating your software will fix the computer glitch.

b. The challenge in decreasing the town budget is identifying nonessential services.

c. Cathleen tried to help her mother by raking the lawn.

d. Understanding little, I had no hope of passing my biology final.

e. Working with animals gave Steve a sense of satisfaction.

1. Driving through Leamington, we saw kudzu growing out of control along the roadside.

2. Some people now use a patch to repel mosquitoes.

3. We helped the schoolchildren find their way to the station.

4. Painting requires the ability to keep a steady hand.

5. My father could not see a weed without pulling it out of the ground.

Hacker/Sommers, *Exercises for A Canadian Writer's Reference*, 5th ed. (Boston: Bedford, 2012)

EXERCISE B3-3 ◆ Subordinate word groups: subordinate clauses

Before working this exercise, read section B3-e in *A Canadian Writer's Reference*, Fifth Edition.

Underline the subordinate clauses in the following sentences. Tell whether each clause is an adjective, adverb, or noun clause and how it is used in the sentence. Answers to lettered sentences appear in the back of the booklet. Example:

> **Show the committee the latest draft <u>before you print the final report</u>.** *(Adverb clause modifying "Show")*

a. The city's electoral commission adjusted the voting process so that every vote would count.

b. A marketing campaign that targets baby boomers may not appeal to young professionals.

c. After the Tambora volcano erupted in the southern Pacific in 1815, no one realized that it would contribute to the "year without a summer" in Europe and North America.

d. The concept of peak oil implies that at a certain point there will be no more oil to extract from the earth.

e. Details are easily overlooked when you are rushing.

1. What her internship taught her was that she worked well with children with special needs.

2. Whether you like it or not, you cannot choose your family.

3. The meteorologist who underestimated the total snowfall of the first winter storm was right on target about the second storm.

4. If Ramon didn't have to work every afternoon, he would be willing to sign up for the yoga class with Andrea.

5. The book that we saw in the shop in Dublin was not available when we returned home.

Hacker/Sommers, *Exercises for A Canadian Writer's Reference*, 5th ed. (Boston: Bedford, 2012)

B3-3 | Subordinate word groups: subordinate clauses   **95**

EXERCISE B4-1 ◆ Sentence types

Before working this exercise, read section B4 in *A Canadian Writer's Reference*, Fifth Edition.

Identify the following sentences as simple, compound, complex, or compound-complex. Identify the subordinate clauses and classify them according to their function: adjective, adverb, or noun. (See B3-e.) Answers to lettered sentences appear in the back of the booklet. Example:

> **The deli in Courthouse Square was crowded with lawyers at lunchtime.** *(Simple)*

a. Fires that are ignited in dry areas spread especially quickly.

b. The early Incas were advanced; they used a calendar and developed a decimal system.

c. Elaine's jacket was too thin to block the wintry air.

d. Before we leave for the station, we always check the Via Rail Web site.

e. Decide when you want to leave, and I will be there to pick you up.

1. The fact is that the network outage could have been avoided.

2. Those who lose a loved one in a tragic accident may find group therapy comforting.

3. The outlets in the fashion district are the best places to find Halloween costumes.

4. There were six lunar Apollo missions, but people usually remember Apollo 13 best.

5. Our generator kicks in whenever we lose power.

Hacker/Sommers, *Exercises for A Canadian Writer's Reference*, 5th ed. (Boston: Bedford, 2012)

Answers to Lettered Exercises

Sentence Style

EXERCISE S1-1, page 1

Possible revisions:

a. Police dogs are used for finding lost children, tracking criminals, and detecting bombs and illegal drugs.
b. Hannah told her rock-climbing partner that she bought a new harness and that she wanted to climb Mount McConnell.
c. It is more difficult to sustain an exercise program than to start one.
d. During basic training, I was told not only what to do but also what to think.
e. Jan wanted to drive to the wine country or at least to the Niagara Escarpment.

EXERCISE S2-1, page 2

Possible revisions:

a. A grapefruit or an orange is a good source of vitamin C.
b. The women entering RMC can expect haircuts as short as those of the male cadets.
c. Looking out the family room window, Sarah saw that her favourite tree, which she had climbed as a child, was gone.
d. The graphic designers are interested in and knowledgeable about producing posters for the balloon race.
e. Reefs are home to more species than any other ecosystem in the sea.

EXERCISE S3-1, page 3

Possible revisions:

a. More research is needed to evaluate effectively the risks posed by volcanoes in the Pacific Northwest.
b. Many students graduate from university with debt totalling more than twenty thousand dollars.
c. It is a myth that humans use only 10 percent of their brains.
d. A coolhunter is a person who can find the next wave of fashion in the unnoticed corners of modern society.
e. Not all geese fly beyond Kamloops for the winter.

EXERCISE S3-2, page 4

Possible revisions:

a. Though Martha was only sixteen, UBC accepted her application.
b. To replace the gear mechanism, you can use the attached form to order the part by mail.
c. As I settled in the cockpit, the pounding of the engine was muffled only slightly by my helmet.
d. After studying polymer chemistry, Phuong found computer games less complex.
e. When I was a young man, my mother enrolled me in tap dance classes.

EXERCISE S4-3, page 7

Possible revisions:

a. A talented musician, Julie Crochetière uses R&B, soul, and jazz styles. She even performs pop music well.
b. Environmentalists point out that shrimp farming in Southeast Asia is polluting water and making farmlands useless. They warn that governments must act before it is too late.
c. We observed the samples for five days before we detected any growth. *Or* The samples were observed for five days before any growth was detected.

d. In his famous soliloquy, Hamlet contemplates whether death would be preferable to his difficult life and, if so, whether he is capable of committing suicide.
e. The lawyer told the judge that Miranda Hale was innocent and asked that she be allowed to prove the allegations false. *Or* The lawyer told the judge, "Miranda Hale is innocent. Please allow her to prove the allegations false."

EXERCISE S4-4, page 8

Possible revisions:

a. Courtroom lawyers have more than a touch of theatre in their blood.
b. The interviewer asked if we had brought our proof of citizenship and our passports.
c. Reconnaissance scouts often have to make fast decisions and use sophisticated equipment to keep their teams from being detected.
d. After the animators finish their scenes, the production designer arranges the clips according to the storyboard and makes synchronization notes for the sound editor and the composer.
e. Madame Defarge is a sinister figure in Dickens's *A Tale of Two Cities*. On a symbolic level, she represents fate; like the Greek Fates, she knits the fabric of individual destiny.

EXERCISE S5-1, page 9

Possible revisions:

a. Using surgical gloves is a precaution now taken by dentists to prevent contact with patients' blood and saliva.
b. A career in medicine, which my brother is pursuing, requires at least ten years of challenging work.
c. The pharaohs had bad teeth because tiny particles of sand found their way into Egyptian bread.
d. Recurring bouts of flu caused the team to forfeit a record number of games.
e. This box contains the key to your future.

EXERCISE S6-1, page 11

Possible revisions:

a. In 1987, Jenkins was elected to the Canadian Baseball Hall of Fame, and he was the first Canadian elected to the Baseball Hall of Fame in Cooperstown, New York.
b. Jenkins was the first Canadian pitcher to win the Cy Young Award; he also won the Lou Marsh Trophy as Canada's outstanding athlete in 1974.
c. Although he was grateful to have won a Cy Young Award, Jenkins felt that he should have won more.
d. Jenkins loved being a baseball pitcher; for example, he told *Baseball Almanac* that he didn't consider pitching to be work.
e. Jenkins pitched six consecutive twenty-win seasons between 1967 and 1972; he will likely be the last pitcher to do it because today's pitchers start fewer games.

EXERCISE S6-2, page 13

Possible revisions:

a. The X-Men comic books and Japanese woodcuts of kabuki dancers, all part of Marlena's research project on popular culture, covered the tabletop and the chairs.
b. Our waitress, costumed in a kimono, had painted her face white and arranged her hair in a lacquered beehive.
c. Students can apply for a spot in the leadership program, which teaches thinking and communication skills.

d. Shore houses were flooded up to the first floor, beaches were washed away, and Brant's Lighthouse was swallowed by the sea.
e. Laura Thackray, an engineer at Volvo Car Corporation, addressed women's safety needs by designing a pregnant crash-test dummy.

EXERCISE S6-3, page 14

Possible revisions:

a. These particles, known as "stealth liposomes," can hide in the body for a long time without detection.
b. Jan, a competitive gymnast majoring in biology, intends to apply her athletic experience and her science degree to a career in sports medicine.
c. Because textile workers and labour unions have loudly pro-tested sweatshop abuses, apparel makers have been forced to examine their labour practices.
d. Developed in a European university, IRC (Internet Relay Chat) was created as a way for a group of graduate students to talk about projects from their dorm rooms.
e. The cafeteria's new menu, which has an international flavour, includes everything from enchiladas and pizza to pad thai and sauerbraten.

EXERCISE S6-4, page 15

Possible revisions:

a. Working as an aide for the relief agency, Gina distributed food and medical supplies.
b. Janbir, who spent every Saturday learning tabla drumming, noticed each week that his memory for complex patterns was growing stronger.
c. When the rotor hit, it gouged a hole about five centimetres deep in my helmet.
d. My grandfather, who was born eighty years ago in Puerto Rico, raised his daughters the old-fashioned way.
e. By reversing the depressive effect of the drug, the Narcan saved the patient's life.

EXERCISE S7-1, page 17

Possible revisions:

a. Across the hall from the fossils exhibit are the exhibits for insects and spiders.
b. After growing up desperately poor in Japan, Sayuri becomes a successful geisha.
c. Researchers who have been studying Mount St. Helens for years believe that a series of earthquakes in the area may have caused the 1980 eruption.
d. Ice cream typically contains 10 percent milk fat, but premium ice cream may contain up to 16 percent milk fat and has con-siderably less air in the product.
e. If home values climb, the economy may recover more quickly than expected.

Word Choice

EXERCISE W1-1, page 20

Possible revisions:

a. The number of gifts a Nootka chief gave at a potlatch indicated his prestige in his tribe.
b. The cat just sat there watching his prey.
c. Correct
d. Correct
e. Chris redesigned the boundary plantings to try to improve the garden's overall design.

EXERCISE W2-1, page 21

Possible revisions:

a. Martin Luther King Jr. set a high standard for future leaders.

b. Alice has loved cooking since she could first peek over a kitchen tabletop.
c. Bloom's race for the premiership is futile.
d. A successful graphic designer must have technical knowledge and an eye for colour and balance.
e. You will deliver mail to all employees.

EXERCISE W3-1, page 23

Possible revisions:

a. The Prussians defeated the Saxons in 1745.
b. Ahmed, the producer, manages the entire operation.
c. The tour guides expertly paddled the sea kayaks.
d. Emphatic and active; no change
e. Protesters were shouting on the courthouse steps.

EXERCISE W4-1, page 24

Possible revisions:

a. In my youth, my family was poor.
b. This conference will help me serve my clients better.
c. The meteorologist warned the public about the possible dan-gers of the coming storm.
d. Government studies show a need for after-school programs.
e. Passengers should try to complete the customs declaration form before leaving the plane.

EXERCISE W4-3, page 26

Possible revisions:

a. Dr. Geralyn Farmer is the chief surgeon at University Hospi-tal. Dr. Paul Green is her assistant.
b. All applicants want to know how much they will earn.
c. Elementary school teachers should understand the concept of nurturing if they intend to be effective.
d. Obstetricians need to be available to their patients at all hours.
e. If we do not stop abusing natural resources and polluting our environment, we will perish.

EXERCISE W5-2, page 29

Possible revisions:

a. We regret this delay; thank you for your patience.
b. Ada's plan is to acquire education and experience to prepare herself for a position as property manager.
c. Roger Federer, the ultimate competitor, has earned millions of dollars just in endorsements.
d. Many people take for granted that public libraries have up-to-date computer systems.
e. The effect of Gao Xinjian's novels on Chinese exiles is hard to gauge.

EXERCISE W5-3, page 30

Possible revisions:

a. Queen Anne was so angry with Sarah Churchill that she refused to see her again.
b. Correct
c. The parade moved off the street and onto the beach.
d. The frightened refugees intend to make the dangerous trek across the mountains.
e. What type of wedding are you planning?

EXERCISE W5-4, page 31

Possible revisions:

a. John stormed into the room like a hurricane.
b. Some people insist that they'll always be available to help, even when they haven't been before.
c. The Blue Jays easily beat the Mets, who were in trouble early in the game today at the Rogers Centre.
d. We ironed out the wrinkles in our relationship.
e. My mother accused me of evading her questions when in fact I was just saying the first thing that came to mind.

Grammatical Sentences

EXERCISE G1-2, page 33

a. One of the main reasons for elephant poaching is the profits received from selling the ivory tusks.
b. Correct
c. A number of students in the seminar were aware of the importance of joining the discussion.
d. Batik cloth from Bali, blue and white ceramics from Delft, and a bocce ball from Turin have made Angelie's room the talk of the dorm.
e. Correct

EXERCISE G2-1, page 34

a. When I get the urge to exercise, I lie down until it passes.
b. Grandmother had driven our new SUV to the sunrise church service on Savage Mountain, so we were left with the station wagon.
c. A pile of dirty rags was lying at the bottom of the stairs.
d. How did the computer know that the gamer had gone from the room with the blue ogre to the hall where the gold was heaped?
e. The computer programmer was an expert in online security; he was confident that the encryption code he used could never be broken.

EXERCISE G2-2, page 35

a. The glass sculptures of the Swan Boats were prominent in the brightly lit lobby.
b. Visitors to the glass museum were not supposed to touch the delicate exhibits.
c. Our church has all the latest technology, even a closed-circuit television.
d. Christos didn't know about Marlo's promotion because he never listens. He is [or He's] always talking.
e. Correct

EXERCISE G2-3, page 36

Possible revisions:

a. Correct
b. Watson and Crick discovered the mechanism that controls inheritance in all life: the workings of the DNA molecule.
c. When city planners proposed rezoning the waterfront, did they know that the mayor had promised to curb development in that neighbourhood?
d. Correct
e. Correct

EXERCISE G3-1, page 37

Possible revisions:

a. Every candidate for prime minister must appeal to a wide variety of ethnic and social groups to win the election.
b. David lent his motorcycle to someone who allowed a friend to use it.
c. The aerobics teacher motioned for all the students to move their arms in wide, slow circles.
d. Correct
e. Applicants should be bilingual if they want to qualify for this position.

EXERCISE G3-3, page 39

Possible revisions:

a. Some professors say that engineering students should have hands-on experience with dismantling and reassembling machines.
b. Because she had decorated her living room with posters from chamber music festivals, her date thought she was interested in classical music. Actually she preferred rock.
c. In my high school, students didn't need to get all A's to be considered a success; they just needed to work to their ability.

d. Marianne told Jenny, "I am worried about your mother's illness." [or ". . . about my mother's illness."]
e. Though Lewis cried for several minutes after scraping his knee, eventually the pain subsided.

EXERCISE G3-5, page 41

a. Correct [But the writer could change the end of the sentence: . . . *than he is.*]
b. Correct [But the writer could change the end of the sentence: . . . *that she was the coach.*]
c. She appreciated his telling the truth in such a difficult situation.
d. The director has asked you and me to draft a proposal for a new recycling plan.
e. Five close friends and I rented a van, packed it with food, and drove two hundred kilometres to the Calgary Stampede.

EXERCISE G3-7, page 43

a. The roundtable featured scholars whom I had never heard of. [or . . . scholars I had never heard of.]
b. Correct
c. Correct
d. Daniel always gives a holiday donation to whoever needs it.
e. So many singers came to the audition that Natalia had trouble deciding whom to select for the choir.

EXERCISE G4-1, page 44

Possible revisions:

a. Did you do well on last week's chemistry exam?
b. With the budget deadline approaching, our office has hardly had time to handle routine correspondence.
c. Correct
d. The customer complained that he hadn't been treated nicely.
e. Of all my relatives, Uncle Roberto is the cleverest.

EXERCISE G5-1, page 46

Possible revisions:

a. Listening to the CD her sister had sent, Mia was overcome with a mix of emotions: happiness, homesickness, and nostalgia.
b. Cortés and his soldiers were astonished when they looked down from the mountains and saw Tenochtitlán, the magnificent capital of the Aztec Empire.
c. Although my spoken French is not very good, I can read the language with ease.
d. There are several reasons for not eating meat. One reason is that dangerous chemicals are used throughout the various stages of meat production.
e. To learn how to sculpt beauty from everyday life is my intention in studying art and archaeology.

EXERCISE G6-1, page 48

Possible revisions:

a. The city had one public swimming pool that stayed packed with children all summer long.
b. The building is being renovated, so at times we have no heat, water, or electricity.
c. The view was not what the travel agent had described. Where were the rolling hills and the shimmering rivers?
d. All those gnarled equations looked like toxic insects; maybe I was going to have to rethink my major.
e. City officials had good reason to fear a major earthquake: Most [or most] of the business district was built on landfill.

EXERCISE G6-2, page 49

Possible revisions:

a. Wind power for the home is a supplementary source of energy that can be combined with electricity, gas, or solar energy.
b. Correct

c. In the Middle Ages, when the streets of London were dangerous places, it was safer to travel by boat along the Thames.
d. "He's not drunk," I said. "He's in a state of diabetic shock."
e. Are you able to endure extreme angle turns, high speeds, frequent jumps, and occasional crashes? Then supermoto racing may be a sport for you.

Multilingual Writers and ESL Challenges

EXERCISE M1-1, page 51

a. In the past, tobacco companies denied any connection between smoking and health problems.
b. There is nothing in the world that TV has not touched on.
c. I want to register for a summer tutoring session.
d. By the end of the year, the province will have tested 139 birds for avian flu.
e. The benefits of eating fruits and vegetables have been promoted by health care providers.

EXERCISE M1-2, page 52

a. Many major league pitchers can throw a baseball over ninety-five miles per hour.
b. The writing centre tutor will help you revise your essay.
c. A reptile must adjust its body temperature to its environment.
d. Correct
e. My uncle, a cartoonist, could sketch a person's face in less than two minutes.

EXERCISE M1-3, page 53

Possible revisions:

a. The electrician might have discovered the broken circuit if she had gone through the modules one at a time.
b. If Verena goes to the meeting, she will be late for work.
c. Whenever there is a fire in our neighbourhood, everybody comes out to watch.
d. Sarah did not understand the terms of her internship.
e. If I lived in Budapest with my cousin Szusza, she would teach me Hungarian cooking.

EXERCISE M1-4, page 54

Possible answers:

a. I enjoy riding my motorcycle.
b. The tutor told Samantha to come to the writing centre.
c. The team hopes to work hard and win the championship.
d. Ricardo and his brothers miss surfing during the winter.
e. The babysitter let Roger stay up until midnight.

EXERCISE M2-1, page 55

a. Doing volunteer work often brings satisfaction.
b. As I looked out the window of the plane, I could see Lions Bay.
c. Melina likes to drink her coffee with lots of cream.
d. Correct
e. I completed my homework assignment quickly.

EXERCISE M3-1, page 57

a. There are some cartons of ice cream in the freezer.
b. I don't use the subway because I am afraid.
c. The prime minister is the most popular leader in my country.
d. We tried to get in touch with the same manager whom we spoke to earlier.
e. Recently there have been a number of earthquakes in Turkey.

EXERCISE M3-2, page 58

Possible revisions:

a. Although freshwater freezes at 0 °C, ocean water freezes at –2 °C.

b. Because we switched cable packages, our channel lineup has changed.
c. The competitor confidently mounted his skateboard.
d. My sister performs the *legong*, a Balinese dance, well.
e. Correct

EXERCISE M4-1, page 59

a. Listening to everyone's complaints all day was irritating.
b. The long flight to Singapore was exhausting.
c. Correct
d. After a great deal of research, the scientist made a fascinating discovery.
e. That blackout was one of the most frightening experiences I've ever had.

EXERCISE M4-2, page 60

a. an attractive new Vietnamese sculpture
b. a dedicated Catholic priest
c. her old blue wool sweater
d. Joe's delicious Scandinavian bread
e. many beautiful antique jewellery boxes

EXERCISE M5-1, page 61

a. Whenever we eat at the Centreville Café, we sit at a small table in the corner of the room.
b. Correct
c. On Thursday, Nancy will attend her first home repair class at the community centre.
d. Correct
e. We decided to go to a restaurant because there was no fresh food in the refrigerator.

Punctuation and Mechanics

EXERCISE P1-1, page 62

a. Alisa brought the injured bird home and fashioned a splint out of Popsicle sticks for its wing.
b. Considered a classic of early animation, *The Adventures of Prince Achmed* used hand-cut silhouettes against coloured backgrounds.
c. If you complete the evaluation form and return it within two weeks, you will receive a free breakfast during your next stay.
d. Correct
e. Roger had always wanted a handmade violin, but he couldn't afford one.

EXERCISE P1-2, page 63

a. J. R. R. Tolkien finished writing his draft of *The Lord of the Rings* trilogy in 1949, but the first book in the series wasn't published until 1954.
b. In the first two minutes of its ascent, the space shuttle had broken the sound barrier and reached a height of over forty kilometres.
c. German shepherds can be gentle guide dogs, or they can be fierce attack dogs.
d. Some former professional cyclists claim that the use of performance-enhancing drugs is widespread in cycling, and they argue that no rider can be competitive without doping.
e. As an intern, I learned most aspects of the broadcasting industry, but I never learned about fundraising.

EXERCISE P1-3, page 64

a. The cold, impersonal atmosphere of the university was unbearable.
b. An ambulance threaded its way through police cars, fire trucks, and curious onlookers.
c. Correct
d. After two broken arms, three cracked ribs, and one concussion, Ken quit the varsity football team.
e. Correct

EXERCISE P1-4, page 65

a. NASA's rovers on Mars are equipped with special cameras that can take close-up, high-resolution pictures of the terrain.
b. Correct
c. Correct
d. Love, vengeance, greed, and betrayal are common themes in Western literature.
e. Many experts believe that shark attacks on surfers are a result of the sharks' mistaking surfboards for small injured seals.

EXERCISE P1-5, page 66

a. Choreographer Louise Bédard's best-known work, *Enfin vous zestes*, is more than just a crowd pleaser.
b. Correct
c. Correct
d. A member of an organization that provides job training for teens was also appointed to the education commission.
e. Brian Eno, who began his career as a rock musician, turned to meditative compositions in the late 1970s.

EXERCISE P1-6, page 67

a. Cricket, which originated in England, is also popular in Australia, South Africa, and India.
b. At the sound of the starting pistol, the horses surged forward toward the first obstacle, a sharp incline one metre high.
c. After seeing an exhibition of Western art, Gerhard Richter escaped from East Berlin and smuggled out many of his notebooks.
d. Corrie's new wet suit has an intricate blue pattern.
e. Correct

EXERCISE P1-7, page 68

a. On January 15, 2008, our office moved to 29 Commonwealth Avenue, Toronto, ON M1K 4J8.
b. Correct
c. Ms. Carlson, you are a valued customer whose satisfaction is very important to us.
d. Mr. Mundy was born on July 22, 1939, in Alberta, where his family had lived for four generations.
e. Correct

EXERCISE P2-1, page 69

a. Correct
b. Tricia's first artwork was a bright blue clay dolphin.
c. Some modern musicians (the group Beyond the Pale is an example) blend several cultural traditions into a unique sound.
d. Myra liked hot, spicy foods such as chili, kung pao chicken, and buffalo wings.
e. On the display screen was a soothing pattern of light and shadow.

EXERCISE P3-1, page 71

a. Do not ask me to be kind; just ask me to act as though I were.
b. If I ever have a conflict between art and nature, I let art win.
c. When I get a little money, I buy books; if any is left, I buy food and clothes.
d. Correct
e. I detest life-insurance agents; they always argue that I shall some day die.

EXERCISE P3-2, page 72

a. Strong black coffee will not sober you up; the truth is that time is the only way to get alcohol out of your system.
b. Margaret was not surprised to see hail and vivid lightning; conditions had been right for violent weather all day.
c. There is often a fine line between right and wrong, good and bad, truth and deception.
d. Correct
e. Severe, unremitting pain is a ravaging force, especially when the patient tries to hide it from others.

EXERCISE P3-3, page 73

a. Correct [Either *It* or *it* is correct.]
b. If we have come to fight, we are far too few; if we have come to die, we are far too many.
c. The travel package includes a round-trip ticket to Athens, a cruise through the Cyclades, and all hotel accommodations.
d. The news article portrays the land use proposal as reckless, although 62 percent of the town's residents support it.
e. Psychologists Kindlon and Thompson (2000) offer parents a simple starting point for raising male children: "Teach boys that there are many ways to be a man" (p. 256).

EXERCISE P4-1, page 74

a. Correct
b. The innovative shoe fastener was inspired by the designer's young grandson.
c. Each day's menu features a different European country's dish.
d. Sue worked overtime to increase her family's earnings.
e. Ms. Jacobs is unwilling to listen to students' complaints about computer failures.

EXERCISE P5-1, page 76

a. As for the advertisement "Sailors have more fun," if you consider chipping paint and swabbing decks fun, then you will have plenty of it.
b. Correct
c. After winning the lottery, Juanita said that she would give half the money to charity.
d. After the movie, Vicki said, "The reviewer called this flick 'trash of the first order.' I guess you can't believe everything you read."
e. Correct

EXERCISE P6-2, page 79

a. A client has left his or her cell phone in our conference room.
b. The films we made of Kilauea on our trip to Hawaii Volcanoes National Park illustrate a typical spatter cone eruption.
c. Correct
d. Correct
e. Of three engineering fields—chemical, mechanical, and materials—Keegan chose materials engineering for its application to toy manufacturing.

EXERCISE P7-2, page 81

a. Correct
b. The swiftly moving tugboat pulled alongside the barge and directed it away from the oil spill in the harbour.
c. Correct
d. Your dog is well known in our neighbourhood.
e. Roadblocks were set up along all the major highways leading out of the city.

EXERCISE P8-1, page 82

a. Assistant Dean Shirin Ahmadi recommended offering more world language courses.
b. Correct
c. Kalindi has an ambitious semester, studying differential calculus, classical Hebrew, brochure design, and Greek literature.
d. Lydia's aunt and uncle make modular houses as beautiful as modernist works of art.
e. We amused ourselves on the long flight by discussing how spring in Kyoto stacks up against summer in London.

EXERCISE P9-1, page 83

a. Correct
b. Some combat soldiers are trained by government diplomats to be sensitive to issues of culture, history, and religion.
c. Correct
d. How many kilograms have you lost since you began lifting weights and adding protein to your diet?
e. Denzil spent all night studying for his psychology exam.

Answers to Lettered Exercises **101**

EXERCISE P9-2, page 84

a. The carpenters located three maple timbers, twenty-one sheets of cherry, and ten oblongs of polished ebony for the theatre set. [In APA and CSE styles, all the numbers would be expressed as numerals.]
b. Correct
c. Correct
d. Eight students in the class won awards at the district art fair.
e. The Canadian National Vimy Memorial in France had 11 285 names inscribed on it when it was unveiled in 1936.

EXERCISE P10-1, page 85

a. Howard Hughes commissioned the *Spruce Goose*, a beautifully built but thoroughly impractical wooden aircraft.
b. The old man screamed his anger, shouting to all of us, "I will not leave my money to you worthless layabouts!"
c. I learned the Latin term *ad infinitum* from an old nursery rhyme about fleas: "Great fleas have little fleas upon their back to bite 'em, / Little fleas have lesser fleas and so on *ad infinitum.*"
d. Correct
e. Neve Campbell's lifelong interest in ballet inspired her involvement in the film *The Company*, which portrays a season with the Joffrey Ballet.

Basic Grammar

EXERCISE B1-1, page 86

a. stage, confrontation, proportions; b. courage, mountain (noun/adjective), climber, inspiration, rescuers; c. need, guest, honour, fog; d. defence (noun/adjective), lawyer, appeal, jury; e. museum, women (noun/adjective), artists, 1987

EXERCISE B1-2, page 87

a. his; b. that, our (pronoun/adjective); c. that, he, himself, some, his (pronoun/adjective); d. I, my (pronoun/adjective), you, one; e. no one, her

EXERCISE B1-3, page 88

a. told; b. were, killed; c. brought down; d. Stay, 'll [will] arrive; e. struggled, was trapped

EXERCISE B1-4, page 89

a. Adjectives: weak, unfocused; b. Adjectives: The (article), Spanish, flexible; adverb: wonderfully; c. Adjectives: The (article), fragrant, the (article), steady; adverb: especially; d. Adjectives: hot, cold; adverbs: rather, slightly, bitterly; e. Adjectives: The (article), its (pronoun/adjective), wicker (noun/adjective); adverb: soundly

EXERCISE B2-1, page 90

a. Complete subjects: The hills and mountains, the snow atop them; simple subjects: hills, mountains, snow; b. Complete subject: points; simple subject: points; c. Complete subject: (You); d. Complete subject: hundreds of fireflies; simple subject: hundreds; e. Complete subject: The evidence against the defendant; simple subject: evidence

EXERCISE B2-2, page 91

a. Subject complement: expensive; b. Direct object: death; c. Direct object: their players' efforts; d. Subject complement: the capital of the Russian Empire; e. Subject complement: bitter

EXERCISE B2-3, page 92

a. Direct objects: adults and children; object complement: weary; b. Direct object: community service; object complement: her priority; c. Direct object: the work; object complement: finished; d. Indirect objects: agent, us; direct objects: our tickets, boarding passes; e. Indirect object: students; direct object: healthy meal choices

EXERCISE B3-1, page 93

a. In northern Italy, as their first language (adverb phrases modifying *speak*); b. through the thick forest (adjective phrase modifying *hike*); with ease (adverb phrase modifying *completed*); c. To my boss's dismay (adverb phrase modifying *was*); for work (adverb phrase modifying *late*); d. of Mayan artifacts (adjective phrase modifying *exhibit*); into pre-Columbian culture (adjective phrase modifying *insight*); e. In 2002, in twelve European countries (adverb phrases modifying *became*)

EXERCISE B3-2, page 94

a. Updating your software (gerund phrase used as subject); b. decreasing the town budget (gerund phrase used as object of the preposition *in*); identifying nonessential services (gerund phrase used as subject complement); c. to help her mother by raking the lawn (infinitive phrase used as direct object); raking the lawn (gerund phrase used as object of the preposition *by*); d. Understanding little (participial phrase modifying *I*); passing my biology final (gerund phrase used as object of the preposition *of*); e. Working with animals (gerund phrase used as subject)

EXERCISE B3-3, page 95

a. so that every vote would count (adverb clause modifying *adjusted*); b. that targets baby boomers (adjective clause modifying *campaign*); c. After the Tambora volcano erupted in the southern Pacific in 1815 (adverb clause modifying *realized*); that it would contribute to the "year without a summer" in Europe and North America (noun clause used as direct object of *realized*); d. that at a certain point there will be no more oil to extract from the earth (noun clause used as direct object of *implies*); e. when you are rushing (adverb clause modifying *are overlooked*)

EXERCISE B4-1, page 96

a. Complex; that are ignited in dry areas (adjective clause); b. Compound; c. Simple; d. Complex; Before we leave for the station (adverb clause); e. Compound-complex; when you want to leave (noun clause)